LOTUS® 1-2-3®
Release 4 for Windows™
Illustrated

LOTUS 1-2-3
Release 4 for Windows
Illustrated

Brenda L. Nielsen
Mesa Community College

Lotus 1-2-3 Release 4 for Windows Illustrated is published by Course Technology, Inc.

Vice President, Publisher	Joseph B. Dougherty
Managing Editor	Marjorie Schlaikjer
Director of Production	Myrna D'Addario
Production Editor	Roxanne Alexander
Composition	Gex, Inc.
Copyeditor	Christy Barbee
Proofreader	Jane Pedicini
Indexer	Alexandra Nickerson
Product Testing and Support Supervisor	Jeff Goding
Technical Reviewers	Thomas Kutter
	James Valente
	Mark Vodnik
Prepress Production	Gex, Inc.
Manufacturing Manager	Elizabeth Martinez
Instructional Designer	Debbie Krivoy
Text Designer	Leslie Hartwell
Cover Designer	John Gamache
Technical Writers	P.A.M. Borys, Marjorie Schlaikjer

Lotus 1-2-3 Release 4 for Windows Illustrated © 1994 Course Technology, Inc.

Trademarks

Course Technology and the open book logo are registered trademarks of Course Technology, Inc.

Lotus 1-2-3 is a registered trademark of Lotus Development Corporation and Windows is a registered trademark of Microsoft Corporation.

Some of the product names used in this book have been used for identification purposes only and may be trademarks or registered trademarks of their respective manufacturers and sellers.

Disclaimer

Course Technology, Inc. reserves the right to revise this publication and make changes from time to time in its content without notice.

ISBN 1-56527-168-8

Printed in the United States of America

10 9 8 7 6 5 4 3

From the Publisher

At Course Technology, Inc., we believe that technology will transform the way that people teach and learn. We are very excited about bringing you, college professors and students, the most practical and affordable technology-related products available.

The Course Technology Development Process

Our development process is unparalleled in the higher education publishing industry. Every product we create goes through an exacting process of design, development, review, and testing.

Reviewers give us direction and insight that shape our manuscripts and bring them up to the latest standards. Every manuscript is quality tested. Students whose background matches the intended audience work through every keystroke, carefully checking for clarity, and pointing out errors in logic and sequence. Together with our technical reviewers, these testers help us ensure that everything that carries our name is error-free and easy to use.

Course Technology Products

We show both *how* and *why* technology is critical to solving problems in college and in whatever field you choose to teach or pursue. Our time-tested, step-by-step instructions provide unparalleled clarity. Examples and applications are chosen and crafted to motivate students.

The Course Technology Team

This book will suit your needs because it was delivered quickly, efficiently, and affordably. In every aspect of business, we rely on a commitment to quality and the use of technology. Every employee contributes to this process. The names of all our employees are listed below: Tim Ashe, David Backer, Stephen M. Bayle, Josh Bernoff, Erin Bridgeford, Ann Marie Buconjic, Jody Buttafoco, Jim Chrysikos, Susan Collins, John M. Connolly, David Crocco, Myrna D'Addario, Lisa D'Alessandro, Howard S. Diamond, Kathryn Dinovo, Katie Donovan, Joseph B. Dougherty, MaryJane Dwyer, Chris Elkhill, Don Fabricant, Kate Gallagher, Laura Ganson, Jeff Goding, Laurie Gomes, Eileen Gorham, Andrea Greitzer, Tim Hale, Roslyn Hooley, Tom Howes, Nicole Jones, Matt Kenslea, Suzanne Licht, Kim Mai, Elizabeth Martinez, Debbie Masi, Dan Mayo, Kathleen McCann, Jay McNamara, Mac Mendelsohn, Laurie Michelangelo, Kim Munsell, Amy Oliver, Kristine Otto, Debbie Parlee, Kristin Patrick, Charlie Patsios, Jodi Paulus, Darren Perl, Kevin Phaneuf, George J. Pilla, Cathy Prindle, Nancy Ray, Marjorie Schlaikjer, Christine Spillett, Susan Stroud, Michelle Tucker, David Upton, Mark Valentine, Renee Walkup, Lisa Yameen.

Preface

Course Technology, Inc. is proud to present this new book in its Illustrated Series. *Lotus 1-2-3 Release 4 for Windows Illustrated* provides a highly visual, hands-on introduction to Lotus 1-2-3. The book is designed as a learning tool for Lotus 1-2-3 novices but will also be useful as a source for future reference.

Organization and Coverage

Lotus 1-2-3 Release 4 for Windows Illustrated contains a Windows overview and eight units that cover basic Lotus 1-2-3 skills. In these units students learn how to plan, build, edit, and enhance 1-2-3 worksheets. The book also covers creating charts, creating and managing a database, and recording and running macros.

Approach

Lotus 1-2-3 Release 4 for Windows Illustrated distinguishes itself from other textbooks with its highly visual approach to computer instruction.

Lessons: Information Displays

The basic lesson format of this text is the "information display," a two-page lesson that is sharply focused on a specific task. This sharp focus and the precise beginning and end of a lesson make it easy for students to study specific material. Modular lessons are less overwhelming for students, and they provide instructors with more flexibility in planning classes and assigning specific work.

Each lesson, or "information display," contains the following elements:

Introduction — Concise text that introduces the basic principles discussed in the lesson and integrates the brief case study scenario. Procedures are easier to learn when concepts fit into a framework.

Numbered steps — Clear step-by-step directions explain how to complete the specific task. When students follow the numbered steps, they quickly learn how each procedure is performed and what the results will be.

Reference tables — These are quickly accessible summaries of key terms, SmartIcon shortcuts, or keyboard alternatives connected with the lesson material. Students can refer easily to this information when working on their own projects at a later time.

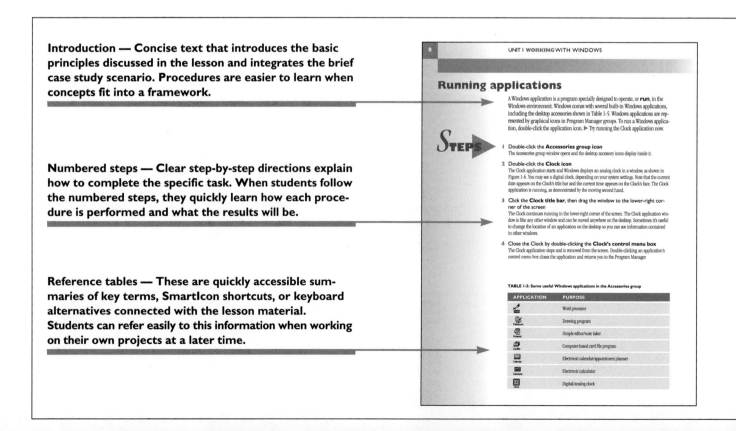

Features

Lotus 1-2-3 Release 4 for Windows Illustrated is an exceptional textbook because it contains the following features:

- "Read This Before You Begin" Page — This page provides essential information that both students and instructors need to know before they begin working through the units. Information about the Student Disk is listed in one place to help students and instructors save time and aggravation.

- Windows Overview — A "Working with Windows" overview is provided in Unit 1 so students can begin working in the Windows environment right away. This unit introduces students to the graphical user interface and helps them learn basic skills they can use in all Windows applications.

- Real-World Case — The case study used throughout the textbook is designed to be "real-world" in nature and representative of the kinds of activities that students will encounter when working with spreadsheet applications. With a real-world case, the process of solving the problem will be more meaningful to students.

- End of Unit Material — Each unit concludes with a meaningful Concepts Review that tests students' understanding of what they learned in the unit. The Concepts Review is followed by an Applications Review, which provides students with additional hands-on practice of the skills they learned in the unit. The Applications Review is followed by an Independent Challenge, which poses an open-ended, real-world case problem for students to solve. The Independent Challenge allows students to learn by exploring, and develops critical thinking skills.

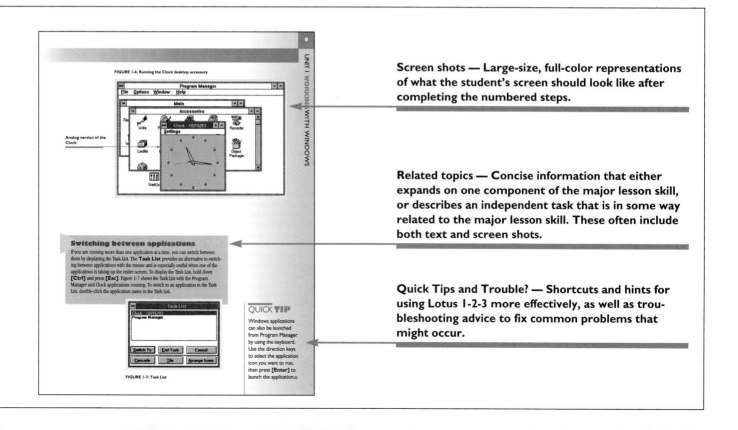

Screen shots — Large-size, full-color representations of what the student's screen should look like after completing the numbered steps.

Related topics — Concise information that either expands on one component of the major lesson skill, or describes an independent task that is in some way related to the major lesson skill. These often include both text and screen shots.

Quick Tips and Trouble? — Shortcuts and hints for using Lotus 1-2-3 more effectively, as well as troubleshooting advice to fix common problems that might occur.

The Student Disk

The Student Disk bundled with the instructor's copy of this book contains all the data files students need to complete the step-by-step lessons.

Adopters of this text are granted the right to post the Student Disk on any standalone computer or network used by students who have purchased this product.

For more information on the Student Disk, see the section in this book called "Read This Before You Begin."

The Supplements

Instructor's Manual — The Instructor's Manual is *written by the design team* and is quality-assurance tested. It includes:

- Answers and solutions to all lessons, Concept Reviews, Application Reviews, and Independent Challenges
- A disk containing solutions to all of the lessons, Concept Reviews, Application Reviews, and Independent Challenges
- Unit notes, which contain tips from the author about the instructional progression of each lesson
- Transparency masters of key concepts

Test Bank — The Test Bank contains 50 questions per unit in true/false, multiple choice, and fill-in-the-blank formats, plus 2 essay questions. Each question has been quality assurance tested by students to achieve clarity and accuracy.

Electronic Test Bank — The Electronic Test Bank allows instructors to edit individual test questions, select questions individually or at random, and print out scrambled versions of the same test to any supported printer.

Acknowledgments

There are a number of people whose insight and energy have been critical to the success of this project. Thanks go to Joe Dougherty for providing the vision and opportunity to produce the Illustrated series, to Leslie Hartwell for a terrific textbook design, to Roxanne Alexander for superb production editing, to P.A.M. Borys for technical writing, to Debbie Krivoy for outstanding instructional design, to Marjorie Schlaikjer for valuable developmental review and consultation, and to Mike Halvorson for creating a solid Windows overview.

Brief Contents

Contents

TABLES

Read This Before You Begin

To the Student

The exercises and examples in this book feature several ready-made Lotus 1-2-3 worksheet files which are contained on the Student Disk provided to your instructor. To complete the step-by-step exercises in this book, you must have a Student Disk. Your instructor will either provide you with your own copy of the Student Disk or will make the Student Disk files available to you over a network in your school's computer lab. See your instructor or lab manager for further information.

Using your own computer

If you are going to work through this book using your own computer, you need a computer system running Microsoft Windows 3.1, Lotus 1-2-3 Release 4 or 4.01 for Windows (commercial or student version), and a Student Disk. *You will not be able to complete the step-by-step exercises in this book using your own computer until you have your own Student Disk.*

To the Instructor

Bundled with the instructor's copy of this book is the Student Disk, which contains all the files your students need to complete the step-by-step exercises and the end-of-unit review material in this book. Adopters of this text are granted the right to distribute the files on the Student Disk to any student who has purchased a copy of this text. You are free to post all these files to a network or standalone workstations, or simply provide copies of the disk to your students. The instructions in this book assume that the students know which drive and directory contain the Student Disk files, so it's important that you provide disk location information before the students start working through the units. You also need to provide instructions about where students should save their modified files.

Using the Student Disk files

To keep the original files on the Student Disk intact, the instructions in this book for opening files require two important steps: (1) Open the existing file and (2) Save it as a new file with a new name. This procedure ensures that the original file will remain unmodified in case the student wants to redo the exercise. For more information about opening and renaming files, please refer to the lesson "Opening an existing worksheet" in Unit 4.

UNIT 1

Working WITH WINDOWS

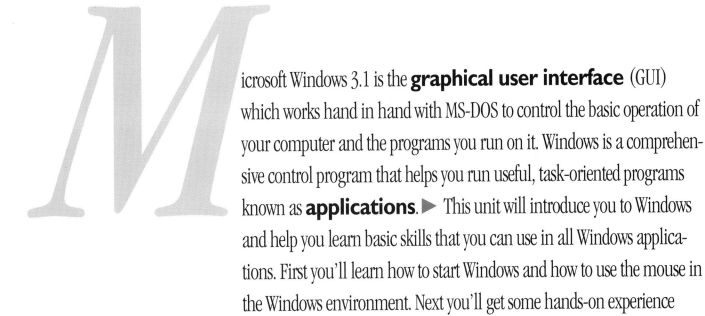

icrosoft Windows 3.1 is the **graphical user interface** (GUI) which works hand in hand with MS-DOS to control the basic operation of your computer and the programs you run on it. Windows is a comprehensive control program that helps you run useful, task-oriented programs known as **applications**. ▶ This unit will introduce you to Windows and help you learn basic skills that you can use in all Windows applications. First you'll learn how to start Windows and how to use the mouse in the Windows environment. Next you'll get some hands-on experience with Program Manager and you'll learn how to work with groups, run applications, resize windows, and use menus and commands. Then you'll learn how to exit a Windows application and exit Windows itself. ▶

Starting Windows

Windows is started, or **launched**, from MS-DOS with the **win** command. Once started, it takes over most of the duties of MS-DOS and provides a graphical environment for you to run your programs in. Windows has several advantages over MS-DOS. As a graphical interface, it uses meaningful pictures and symbols known as icons to replace hard-to-remember commands. Windows lets you run more than one application at a time, so you can run, for example, a word processor and a spreadsheet at the same time and easily share data between them. ▶ Each application is represented in a rectangular space called a **window**. The Windows environment also includes several useful desktop accessories, including Clock and Notepad, that you can use for day-to-day tasks. ▶ Try starting Windows now.

1 Turn on your computer

The computer displays some technical information as it starts up and tests its circuitry. MS-DOS loads automatically, then displays the **command prompt** (usually C:\>). The command prompt allows you access to MS-DOS commands and applications.

2 Type win, then press [Enter]

This is the command used to start Windows. (If your computer is set up so that it automatically runs Windows when it starts, then Windows might already be running.)

The screen momentarily goes blank while the computer loads Windows. An hourglass then appears, indicating Windows is getting ready for your first request. Then the Windows Program Manager displays on your screen, as shown in Figure 1-1.

TABLE 1-1:
Elements of the Windows desktop

DESKTOP ELEMENT	DESCRIPTION
Program Manager	The main control program of Windows. All Windows applications are started from the Program Manager.
Window	A framed region on the screen. The Program Manager is framed in a window.
Application icon	The graphic representation of a Windows application.
Title bar	An area directly below the window's top border that displays the window's name.
Sizing buttons	Buttons in the upper-right corner of a window that can be used to minimize or maximize a window.
Menu bar	The area under the title bar on a window. The menu bar provides access to most of an application's commands.
Control menu box	A box in the upper-left corner of a window used to resize or close a window.
Mouse pointer	An arrow indicating the current location of the mouse on the desktop.

FIGURE 1-1: Opening Windows screen

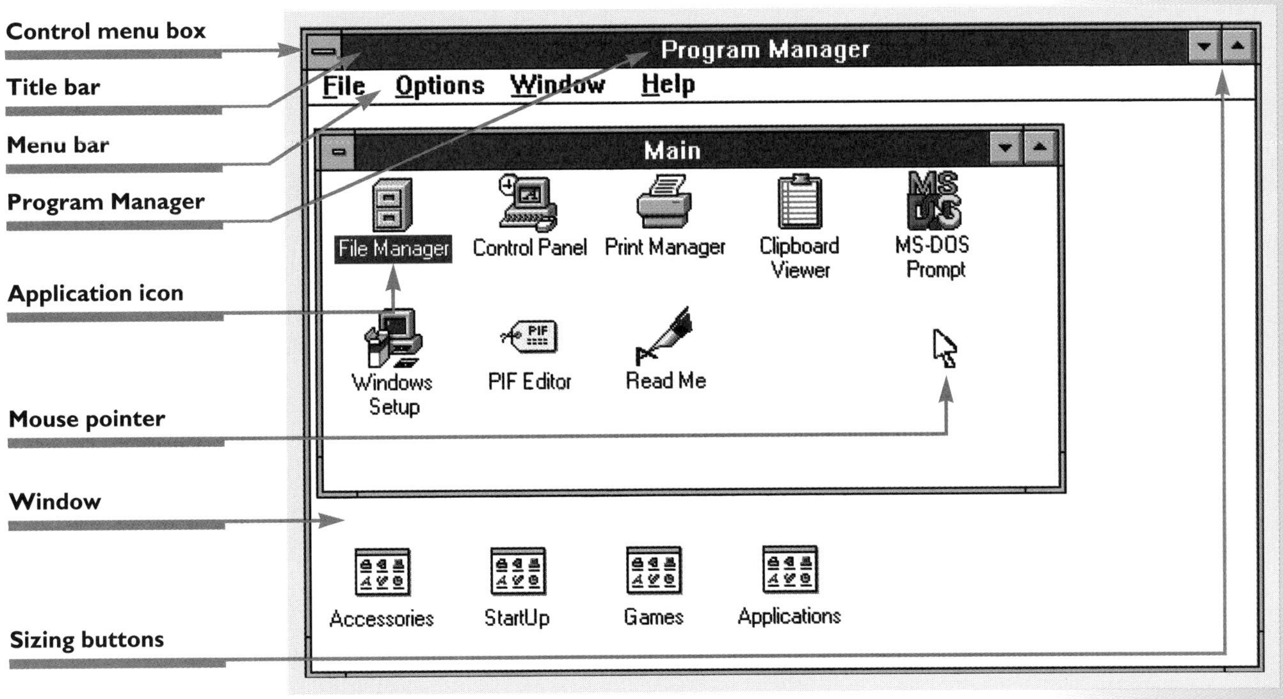

Control menu box

Title bar

Menu bar

Program Manager

Application icon

Mouse pointer

Window

Sizing buttons

Program Manager

File   Options   Window   Help

Main

File Manager   Control Panel   Print Manager   Clipboard Viewer   MS-DOS Prompt

Windows Setup   PIF Editor   Read Me

Accessories   StartUp   Games   Applications

The Windows desktop

The entire screen area on the monitor represents the Windows desktop. The **desktop** is an electronic version of a desk that provides workspace for different computing tasks. Windows allows you to customize the desktop to support the way you like to work and to organize the applications you like to run. Use Table 1-1 to identify the key elements of the desktop, referring to Figure 1-1 for their locations. Because the Windows desktop can be customized, your desktop may look slightly different.

TROUBLE?

If you get an error message when starting Windows, such as Bad command or file name, Windows may not have been properly installed on the computer. Check your Windows documentation for help.

Using the mouse

The **mouse** is a hand-held input device that you roll on your desk to position the mouse pointer on the Windows desktop. When you move the mouse on your desk, the **mouse pointer** on the screen moves in the same direction. The buttons on the mouse are used to select icons and choose commands, and to indicate the work to be done in applications. Table 1-2 lists the four basic mouse techniques. Table 1-3 shows some common mouse pointer shapes. ▶ Try using the mouse now.

I **Locate the mouse pointer on the Windows desktop**
The mouse pointer is in the shape of an arrow and will be located somewhere on the Windows desktop.

2 **Move the mouse on your desk**
Watch how the mouse pointer moves on the Windows desktop in response to your movements. Try moving the mouse pointer in circles, then back and forth in straight lines.

3 **Position the mouse pointer over the Control Panel icon in the Main window in the Program Manager**
Positioning the mouse pointer over an icon is called **pointing**. The Control Panel icon, shown in Figure 1-2, is a graphical representation of the Control Panel application, a special program that controls the operation of the Windows environment. If the Control Panel icon is not visible in the Main window, point at any other icon. The Program Manager is customizable, so the Control Panel could be hidden from view.

4 **Press and release the left mouse button**
Pressing and releasing the mouse button is called **clicking**. When you position the mouse pointer on an icon in Program Manager then click, you **select** the icon. When the Control Panel icon is selected, its title is highlighted, as shown in Figure 1-2.

Now practice a mouse skill called dragging.

5 **With the Control Panel icon selected, hold down the left mouse button and move the mouse down and to the right**
The Control Panel icon moves down and to the right with the mouse pointer, as shown in Figure 1-3. If you release the mouse button, the Control Panel icon will be relocated in the Main window.

6 **Drag the Control Panel icon back to its original position and release the mouse button**

TABLE I-2:
Basic mouse techniques

TECHNIQUE	HOW TO DO IT
Pointing	Move the mouse pointer to a position on the desktop
Clicking	Press and release the mouse button
Double-clicking	Press and release the mouse button twice, quickly
Dragging	Hold down the mouse button and move the mouse to a new location

FIGURE 1-2: Selecting an icon

Highlighted icon title

Main window

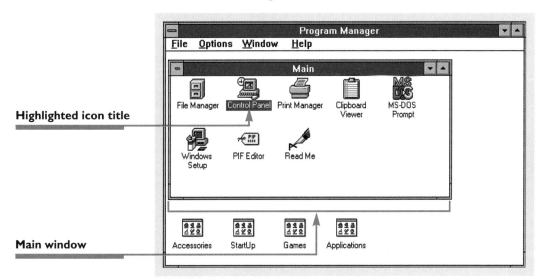

FIGURE 1-3: Dragging an icon

Mouse pointer on
Control Panel

Outline of the icon as
you drag

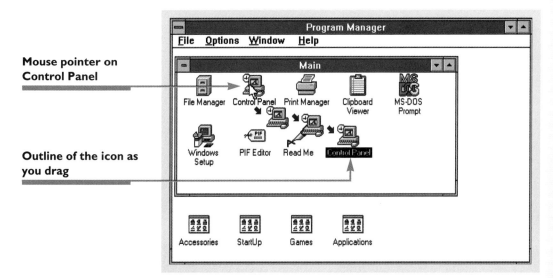

TABLE 1-3: Common mouse pointer shapes

SHAPE	USED TO
↖	Highlight objects, choose commands, start applications, work in applications
I	Position mouse pointer for editing or inserting text; this is called an insertion point
⧖	Indicates Windows is busy processing a command
⟷	Change the size of a window; appears when mouse pointer is on the border of a window

QUICK **TIP**

Windows allows you to modify several characteristics of the mouse, including the double-click rate and the active mouse button (left-handed users may prefer the right button). Ask your instructor for help if you'd like to change the settings for your mouse.■

Using Program Manager groups

Program Manager is where you launch applications and where you organize your applications into windows called groups. A **group** can appear as an open window or as an icon at the bottom of the Program Manager window. Each group has a name related to its contents, and you can reorganize the groups to suit your needs. The standard Windows groups are described in Table 1-4. ▶ Try working with groups now.

I Double-click the Accessories group icon

The Accessories group icon is located at the bottom of the Program Manager window. If you can't locate the Accessories group icon, ask your instructor or lab manager for help. When you double-click the Accessories group icon, it expands into the Accessories group window, as shown in Figure 1-4. Now move the Accessories group window to the right.

2 Click the Accessories group window title bar and drag the group window to the right

A window frame the size of the Accessories group window moves to the right with the mouse. When you release the mouse button, the Accessories group window moves to the location you've indicated. Moving a window lets you see what is beneath it. Any window in the Windows environment can be moved with this technique.

3 Click the title bar of the Main group window

The Main group window becomes the **active window**, the one you are currently working in. Other windows, including the Accessories group window, are considered background windows. Note that the active window also has a highlighted title bar. Program Manager also has a darkened title bar because it is the **active application**.

4 Activate the Accessories group window by clicking anywhere in that window

The Accessories group window moves to the foreground again. Now try closing the Accessories group window to an icon.

5 Double-click the control menu box in the Accessories group window

The control menu box is the small menu in the upper-left corner of the Accessories group window. When you double-click this box, the Accessories group window shrinks to an icon and the Main group window becomes the active window. Double-clicking the control menu box is the easiest way to close any window in the Windows environment.

TABLE I-4:
Standard Windows groups

GROUP NAME	CONTENTS
Main	Applications that control how Windows works; the primary Windows group
Accessories	Useful desktop accessories for day-to-day tasks
StartUp	Programs that run automatically when Windows is started
Games	Game programs for Windows
Applications	A group for applications that are installed later; some applications are installed in their own groups

FIGURE 1-4: Accessories group expanded into a window

Main group window title bar

Control menu box

Accessories group window title bar

Accessories group window

Program Manager group icons

Scroll bars

If a group contains more icons than can be displayed at one time, **scroll bars** appear on the right and/or bottom edges of the window to give you access to the remaining icons, as shown in Figure 1-5. Vertical or horizontal arrows appear at the ends of the bars. To use scroll bars, click the vertical or horizontal arrows that point in the direction you want the window to scroll. Scroll bars appear whenever there is more information than can fit in a window. You'll see them in many Windows applications.

Vertical scroll bar

Scroll arrow

Horizontal scroll bar

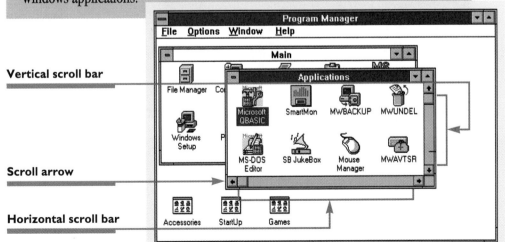

FIGURE 1-5: Vertical and horizontal scroll bars on a window

QUICK **TIP**

Scroll bars can also be operated with the direction keys on the keyboard. To scroll vertically, press [↑] or [↓]. To scroll horizontally, press [←] or [→].■

Running applications

A Windows application is a program specially designed to operate, or **run**, in the Windows environment. Windows comes with several built-in Windows applications, including the desktop accessories shown in Table 1-5. Windows applications are represented by graphical icons in Program Manager groups. To run a Windows application, double-click the application icon. ▶ Try running the Clock application now.

1 Double-click the **Accessories group icon**
The Accessories group window opens and the desktop accessory icons display inside it.

2 Double-click the **Clock icon**
The Clock application starts and Windows displays an analog clock in a window, as shown in Figure 1-6. You may see a digital clock, depending on your system settings. Note that the current date appears on the Clock's title bar and the current time appears on the Clock's face. The Clock application is running, as demonstrated by the moving second hand.

3 Click the **Clock title bar**, then drag the window to the lower-right corner of the screen
The Clock continues running in the lower-right corner of the screen. The Clock application window is like any other window and can be moved anywhere on the desktop. Sometimes it's useful to change the location of an application on the desktop so you can see information contained in other windows.

4 Close the Clock by double-clicking the **Clock's control menu box**
The Clock application stops and is removed from the screen. Double-clicking an application's control menu box closes the application and returns you to the Program Manager.

TABLE 1-5: Some useful Windows applications in the Accessories group

APPLICATION	PURPOSE
Write	Word processor
Paintbrush	Drawing program
Notepad	Simple editor/note taker
Cardfile	Computer-based card file program
Calendar	Electronic calendar/appointment planner
Calculator	Electronic calculator
Clock	Digital/analog clock

FIGURE 1-6: Running the Clock desktop accessory

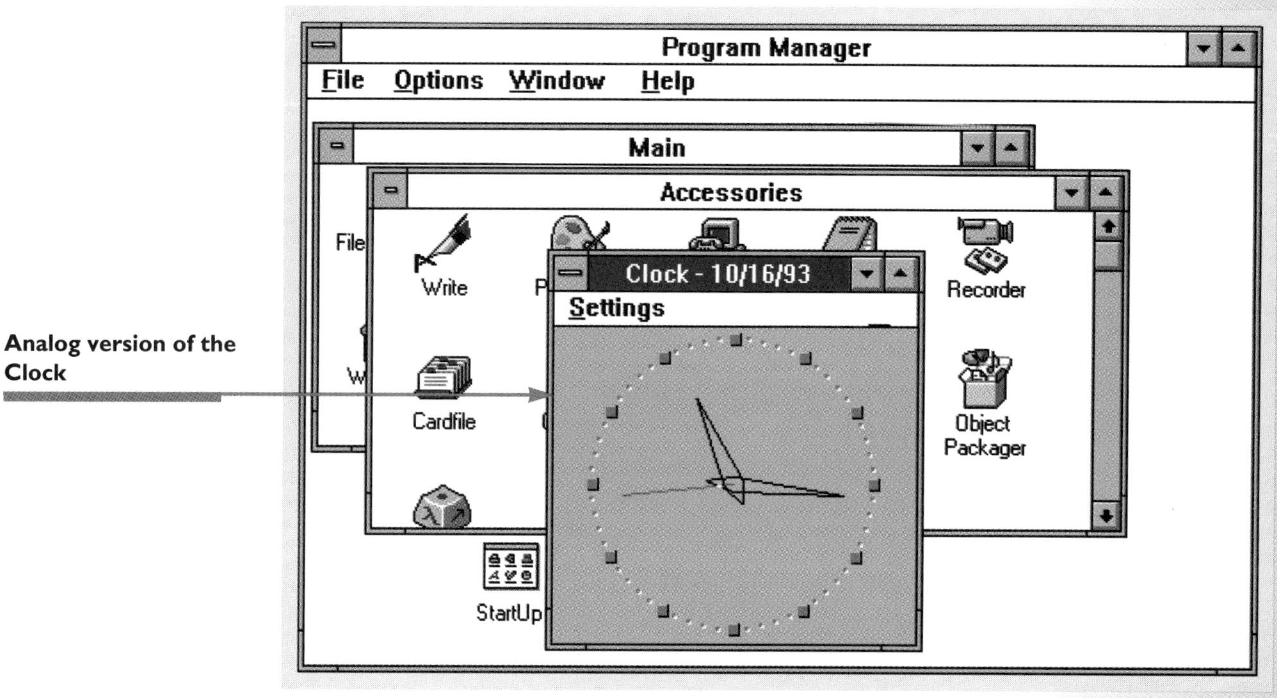

Analog version of the
Clock

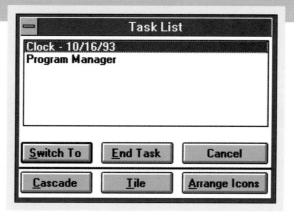

Switching between applications

If you are running more than one application at a time, you can switch between them by displaying the Task List. The **Task List** provides an alternative to switching between applications with the mouse and is especially useful when one of the applications is taking up the entire screen. To display the Task List, hold down **[Ctrl]** and press **[Esc]**. Figure 1-7 shows the Task List with the Program Manager and Clock applications running. To switch to an application in the Task List, double-click the application name in the Task List.

FIGURE 1-7: Task List

QUICK **TIP**

Windows applications can also be launched from Program Manager by using the keyboard. Use the direction keys to select the application icon you want to run, then press **[Enter]** to launch the application.■

Resizing windows

The Windows desktop can get cluttered with icons and windows if you use lots of applications. Each window is surrounded by a standard border and sizing buttons that allow you to minimize, maximize, and restore windows as needed. The sizing buttons are shown in Table 1-6. You'll find they will help you keep the desktop organized. ▶ Try sizing the Clock application window now.

STEPS

1 Start the Clock application by double-clicking the **Clock icon** in the Accessories group

2 Click the **Minimize button** in the upper-right corner of the Clock application

The Minimize button is the sizing button on the left, the one shaped like a down arrow. When you minimize the Clock, it shrinks to an icon at the bottom of the screen, as shown in Figure 1-8. Notice that the Clock icon continues to show the right time, even as an icon. Windows applications continue to run when they are minimized as icons.

3 Double-click the **Clock icon** to restore the Clock application to its original size

The Clock application is restored to its original size and continues to run.

4 Click the **Maximize button** in the upper-right corner of the Clock application

The Maximize button is the sizing button to the right of the Minimize button and is shaped like an up arrow. When you maximize the Clock, it takes up the entire screen, as shown in Figure 1-9. Although it's unlikely you'll want to run the Clock this big very often, you'll find the ability to maximize other Windows applications very useful.

5 Click the **Restore button** in the upper-right corner of the Clock application

The Restore button is the button with up and down arrows and is located to the right of the Minimize button after an application has been maximized. The Restore button returns an application to its original size. See Figure 1-9.

6 Double-click the **Clock control menu box** to close the Clock application

TABLE 1-6:
Buttons for managing windows

BUTTON	PURPOSE
▼	Minimizes an application to an icon on the bottom of the screen
▲	Maximizes an application to its largest possible size
⬍	Restores an application, returning it to its original size

FIGURE 1-8:
Minimized Clock
application as an icon

Minimize button

Maximize button

Minimized Clock with
current time and date

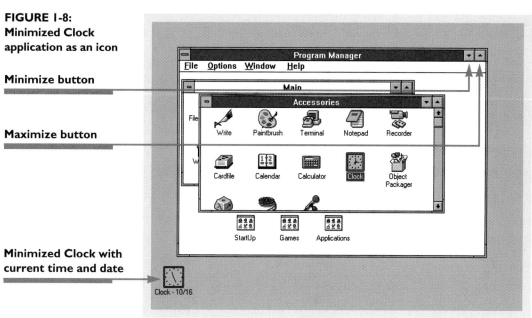

FIGURE 1-9:
Maximized Clock
application filling
entire screen

Restore button

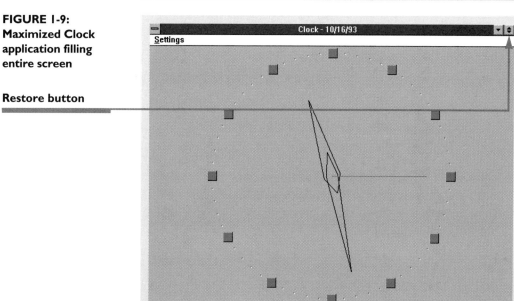

Changing the dimension of a window

The dimension of a window can also be changed, but the window must always be a rectangle. To change the dimension of a window, position the mouse pointer on the window border you want to modify. The mouse pointer changes to ⟨⇔⟩. Drag the border in the direction you want to change. Figure 1-10 shows the height of the Clock window being increased, which will make the Clock face larger.

FIGURE 1-10: Increasing the height of the Clock window

Using menus and commands

The area under the title bar on a window is known as the **menu bar**. The menu bar provides access to most of an application's features through directives known as **commands**. Related commands are listed together in **pull-down menus** and can be executed with the mouse or keyboard. Table 1-7 describes typical items on a menu. ▶ If a menu command name is followed by an ellipsis (...), choosing it will cause a dialog box to display. A **dialog box** is a special window an application displays when more information is needed to execute a command. ▶ Try working with menus and commands in the Notepad application now.

1 Open the **Accessories group window**

2 Start the Notepad application by double-clicking the **Notepad icon**
The Notepad application starts and appears in a window. Notepad is a simple text editor that lets you create memos, record notes, or edit text files. A **text file** is a document containing words, letters, or numbers but no special computer instructions.

Enter some text in Notepad now.

3 Type **Today I started working with Notepad** then press **[Enter]**
The text you type appears on the first line of the Notepad window. The Notepad application contains several of the features of a simple word processor and can process several hundred lines of text.

Next add the current date and time to your text file.

4 Click **Edit** on the Notepad menu bar
The contents of the Edit menu display, as shown in Figure 1-11. The Edit menu includes commands that are useful in word processing. Commands that appear in dimmed type are not available in the current situation. Commands with trailing ellipses indicate a dialog box will be displayed if you choose the command. For a complete list of menu items, see Table 1-7.

Now enter the time and date.

5 Click **Edit** on the Notepad menu bar, then click **Time/Date**
The current time and date appear on the second line of the Notepad window, as shown in Figure 1-12. The Time/Date command is useful for recording the time you accomplish a task.

Now practice opening the other menus in Notepad.

6 Double-click **Notepad's control menu box** to exit Notepad
The Notepad application prepares to close and displays a dialog box that asks if you would like to save the changes (the document) you have created.

7 Click **No** to discard the document you have created
Notepad closes and returns you to Program Manager.

FIGURE 1-11: Notepad's Edit menu

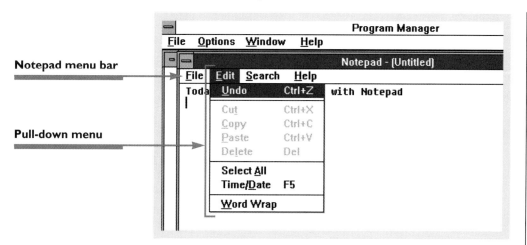

Notepad menu bar

Pull-down menu

FIGURE 1-12: Results of the Time/Date command

Control menu box

Time/Date command

Notepad window

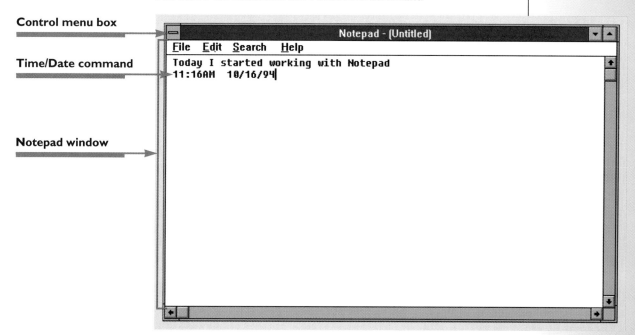

TABLE 1-7: Typical items on a menu

ITEM	MEANING	EXAMPLE
Dimmed command	Command is not currently available	Undo
Ellipsis	Choosing this command will open a dialog box that asks for further information	Paste Special...
Triangle	Clicking this button opens a cascading menu containing an additional list of commands	Axis ▶
Keyboard shortcut	A keyboard alternative for executing a command	Cut Ctrl+X
Underlined letter	Pressing [Alt] and the underlined letter executes this command	Copy Right

Exiting Windows

When you are finished working with Windows, close all the applications you are running and exit Windows by clicking the Exit Windows command on the File menu in the Program Manager window. Do not turn off the computer while Windows is running; you could lose important data if you turn off your computer too soon. ▶ Now try closing all your active applications and exiting Windows.

1 Close any active applications by double-clicking the application's **control menu box**

The application will close. If you have any unsaved changes in your application, a dialog box will ask if you want to save or discard them.

2 Click **File** on the Program Manager menu bar

The File menu displays as shown in Figure 1-13.

3 Click **Exit Windows**

Program Manager displays the Exit Windows dialog box, as shown in Figure 1-14. Dialog boxes appear when you choose a command that is followed by an ellipsis(...). You must respond to the dialog box before the command can be executed. You have two options at this point: Click OK to exit Windows, or click Cancel to abort the Exit Windows command and return to the Program Manager.

4 Click **OK** to exit Windows

Windows finishes its work and the MS-DOS command prompt appears. You can now safely turn off the computer.

FIGURE 1-13: Exiting Windows using the File menu

Menu bar

Exit Windows command

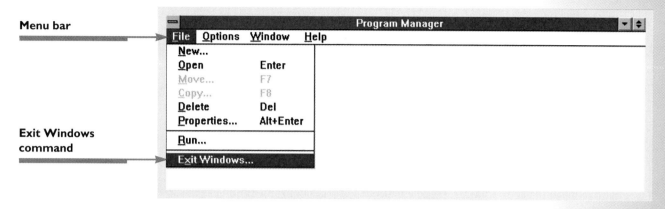

FIGURE 1-14: Exit Windows dialog box

Exiting Windows with the Program Manager control menu box

You can also exit Windows by double-clicking the control menu box in the upper-left corner of the Program Manager window, as shown in Figure 1-15. After you double-click the control menu box, you see the Exit Windows dialog box. Click **OK** to exit Windows.

Double-click the control menu box

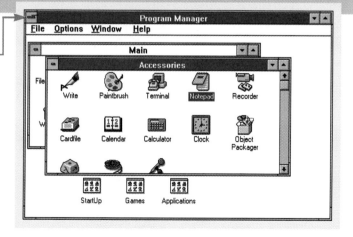

FIGURE 1-15: Exiting Windows with the Program Manager control menu box

TROUBLE?

If you do not exit from Windows before turning off the computer, you may lose data from the applications you used while you were running Windows. Always close your applications and exit from Windows before turning off your computer.■

CONCEPTSREVIEW

Label each of the elements of the Windows screen shown in Figure 1-16.

1 _____

2 _____

3 _____

4 _____

5 _____

6 _____

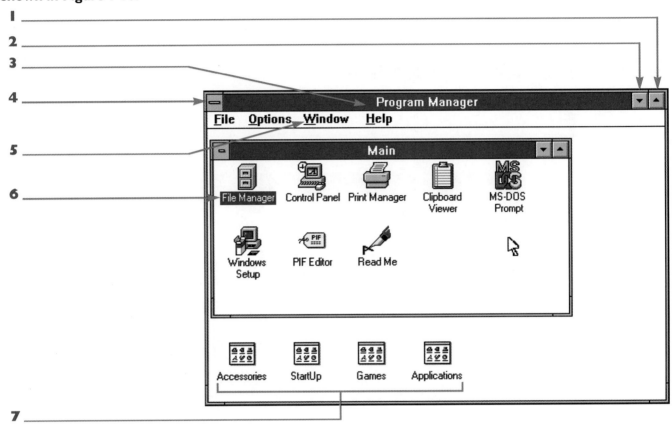

FIGURE 1-16

7 _____

Match each of the statements with the term it describes.

8 Shrinks an application window to the size of an icon

9 Displays the name of the window or application

10 Serves as a launching pad for all applications

11 Expands a window to fill the screen

12 Enables the user to point at screen menus and icons

a. Program Manager

b. Maximize button

c. Mouse

d. Title bar

e. Minimize button

Select the best answer from the list of choices.

13 The acronym GUI means:

a. Grayed user information

b. Group user icons

c. Graphical user interface

d. Group user interconnect

14 The term for starting Windows is:

a. Prompting

b. Launching

c. Applying

d. Processing

15 The small pictures that represent items such as applications are:

a. Icons

b. Windows

c. Buttons

d. Pointers

16 All of the following are examples of using a mouse, EXCEPT:

a. Clicking the Maximize button

b. Pressing [Enter]

c. Pointing at the control menu box

d. Dragging the Games icon

17 When Windows is busy performing a task, the mouse pointer changes to a(n):

a. Hand

b. Arrow

c Clock

d. Hourglass

18 The term for moving an item to a new location on the desktop is:

a. Pointing

b. Clicking

c. Dragging

d. Restoring

19 The Clock, Notepad, and Calendar applications in Windows are known as:

a. Menu commands

b. Control panels

c. Sizing buttons

d. Desktop accessories

20 The Maximize button is used to:

a. Return a window to its original size

b. Expand a window to fill the computer screen

c. Scroll slowly through a window

d. Run programs from the main menu

21 What appears if a window contains more information than can be displayed in the window?

a. Program icon

b. Pull-down menu

c. Scroll bars

d. Check box

22 A window is active when its title bar is:

a. Highlighted

b. Dimmed

c. Checked

d. Underlined

23 What is the term for changing the dimensions of a window?

a. Selecting

b. Resizing

c. Navigating

d. Scrolling

24 The menu bar provides access to an application's functions through:

a. Icons

b. Scroll bars

c. Commands

d. Control menu box

25 You can exit Windows by double-clicking the:

a. Accessories group icon

b. Program Manager control menu box

c. Main window menu bar

d. Control panel application

APPLICATIONS
REVIEW

I Start Windows and identify items on the screen.

   a. Turn on the computer if necessary.

   b. At the command prompt, type WIN, then press [Enter]. After Windows loads, the Program Manager displays.

   c. Try to identify as many items on the worksheet as you can, without referring to the lesson material. Then compare your results with Figure 1-1.

2 Practice using the mouse.

   a. Move the mouse on your desk and watch how the mouse pointer moves on the screen.

   b. Point at the File Manager icon on the Main window. If you cannot locate this icon, point at any other icon.

   c. Click the File Manager icon. Notice that the icon's title is highlighted, as shown in Figure 1-17.

   d. Press and hold down the mouse button, then drag the File Manager icon to the opposite side of the window. Release the mouse button when you are finished moving the icon.

   e. Now drag the icon back to its original location on the desktop.

   f. Practice clicking and dragging other icons on the desktop.

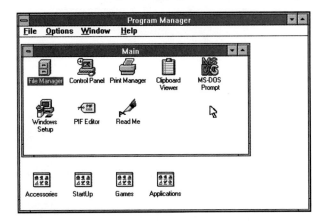

FIGURE I-17

3 Minimize and restore the Program Manager window.

   a. Locate the Minimize button for the Program Manager window.

   b. Click the Minimize button. Notice that the Program Manager window reduces to an icon at the bottom of the screen. Now try restoring the window.

   c. Double-click the minimized Program Manager icon. The Program Manager window opens.

   d. Practice minimizing and restoring other windows on the desktop.

4 Resize and move the Program Manager window.

   a. Click anywhere inside the Program Manger window to activate the window.

   b. Move the mouse pointer over the lower-right corner of the Program Manager window. Notice that the mouse pointer changes to a double-ended arrow.

   c. Press and hold down the mouse button and drag the corner of the window up and to the right until the Program Manager takes up the top third of your screen.

   d. Drag the Program Manager title bar to reposition the window at the bottom of the screen.

5 Practice working with menus.

   a. Using the mouse, pull down the File menu on the Program Manager menu bar. The File menu lists commands you can choose.

   b. Pull down the Options menu on the Program Manager menu bar and review the various menu selections. Notice that each of the Program Manager menus has an underlined letter, indicating a keyboard shortcut.

   c. Now explore the other menus on the Program Manager menu bar. Locate menu commands followed by ellipses (...). This indicates that selecting this command opens a dialog box.

6 Exit Windows.

   a. Close any open application by double-clicking the application's control menu box.

   b. Double-click the control menu box in the upper-left corner of the Program Manager window. The Exit Windows dialog box displays.

   c. Click OK. Windows closes and the DOS command prompt displays.

INDEPENDENT REVIEW

Windows 3.1 provides an on-line tutorial that can help you master essential Windows controls and concepts. The tutorial features interactive lessons that teach you how to use Windows elements such as the mouse, Program Manager, menus, and icons. The tutorial also covers how to use Help.

The tutorial material you should use depends on your level of experience with Windows. Some users may want to review the basics of the Windows work area. Others may want to explore additional Windows topics, such as managing files and customizing windows.

Ask your instructor or lab manager about how to use the Windows on-line tutorial.

UNIT 2

OBJECTIVES

▶ Define spreadsheet software

▶ Start Lotus 1-2-3 for Windows

▶ View the Lotus 1-2-3 screen

▶ Work with menus and dialog boxes

▶ Work with SmartIcons

▶ Get Help

▶ Move around the worksheet

▶ Close a file and exit Lotus 1-2-3

Getting STARTED WITH LOTUS 1-2-3

*N*ow that you have learned some of the basics of Microsoft Windows, you are ready to use Lotus 1-2-3 Release 4 for Windows, a widely used spreadsheet program. In this unit, you will learn how to start Lotus 1-2-3 and recognize and use different elements of the screen and menus. You will also learn the best ways to move around a worksheet and how to use the extensive on-line Help utility. ▶ This unit introduces the All Outdoors Tour and Travel Company. The needs of this business will help you understand many of the ways Lotus 1-2-3 can be used. ▶

Defining spreadsheet software

Lotus 1-2-3 is an **electronic spreadsheet** that runs on DOS, Macintosh and Windows operating systems. An electronic spreadsheet uses a computer's ability to perform numeric calculation rapidly and accurately. Like traditional paper-based spreadsheets, an electronic spreadsheet contains a **worksheet** area that is divided into rows and columns that form individual **cells**. Each cell can contain either text, numbers, formulas or a combination of all three. ► Lucinda Riley works in the accounting department at All Outdoors Tour and Travel Company where they recently switched to Lotus 1-2-3 from a paper-based system. Figure 2-1 shows a budget worksheet that Lucinda created using pencil and paper. Figure 2-2 shows the same worksheet that Lucinda created using Lotus 1-2-3 for Windows. Below are some of the benefits Lucinda gained by switching to an electronic spreadsheet.

■ **Enter data quickly and accurately.** With Lotus 1-2-3, Lucinda can enter information much faster and more accurately than she could using the pencil and paper method. Instead of punching numbers into a calculator and then writing the results into her worksheet, now she only needs to enter data and formulas and Lotus 1-2-3 will calculate the results.

■ **Recalculate easily.** If Lucinda made a mistake using a paper-based system, she had to go back and erase her error and then manually recalculate any changed results. Fixing errors using Lotus 1-2-3 is easy, and all new results based on a changed entry are recalculated automatically.

■ **Perform What-if Analysis.** One of most powerful decision-making features of Lotus 1-2-3 is the ability to change data and then quickly recalculate changed results. Anytime you use a worksheet to answer the question "what if" you are performing a **what-if analysis**. For instance, if the advertising budget for May were increased to $3,000, Lucinda could enter the new figure into the spreadsheet and immediately find out the impact to the overall budget.

■ **Change the appearance of information.** Using a paper-based system, there were limits to how attractive Lucinda could make her worksheets. Lotus 1-2-3 provides powerful features for dressing up a spreadsheet so that information is visual and easy to understand.

■ **Create charts.** Lotus 1-2-3 makes it easy to create charts based on information in a worksheet. Figure 2-2 shows a pie chart that graphically shows the distribution of expenses for the second quarter. Lucinda never created charts when she had a paper-based system. With Lotus 1-2-3 she can create them quickly and easily.

■ **Share information with other users.** Now that everyone at the company is using Lotus 1-2-3, it's easy for Lucinda to share information with her colleagues. If she wants to use the data from someone else's spreadsheet, they can simply give her a disk containing the file.

■ **Create new worksheets from existing ones quickly.** It's now easy for Lucinda to take an existing Lotus 1-2-3 spreadsheet and quickly modify it to create a new one. Using the paper-based system, she always had to start from scratch.

■ **Organize information into a database.** Now Lucinda can take advantage of the database feature in Lotus 1-2-3 to organize information. A **database** is a collection of related information. Lucinda now maintains a database of all employee names and addresses at All Outdoors so that she can keep track of payroll information.

FIGURE 2-1: Traditional paper worksheet

All Outdoors Budget

	Apr	May	Jun	Total
Net Sales	12,000	19,000	16,000	47,000
Expenses				
Salary	2,000	2,000	2,000	6,000
Int	1,200	1,400	1,600	4,200
Rent	600	600	600	1,800
Ads	900	2,000	4,000	6,900
COG	4,000	4,200	5,000	13,200
Total Expense	8,700	10,200	13,200	32,100
Net Income	3,300	8,800	2,800	14,900

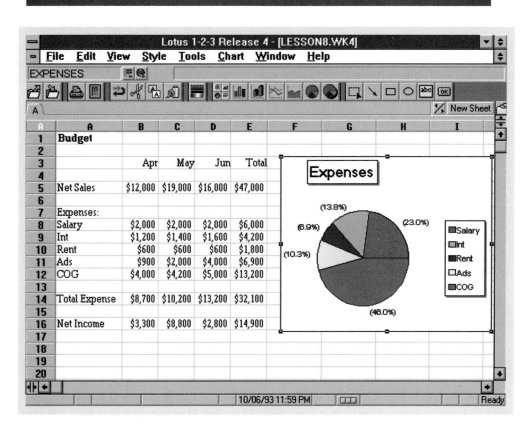

FIGURE 2-2: Lotus 1-2-3 Worksheet and Pie chart

Starting Lotus 1-2-3 for Windows

In most situations, to use Lotus 1-2-3, you must first turn on the computer, access Microsoft Windows from the DOS prompt, then double-click the Lotus 1-2-3 icon. A slightly different procedure may be required for computers on a network and those that use utility programs to enhance Microsoft Windows. ▶ Try starting Lotus 1-2-3 now.

1 Turn on the computer and monitor
The computer may display some technical information. DOS loads into the computer's temporary memory, and then displays the command prompt (C:\>).

2 At the command prompt (c:\>), type win then press [Enter]
The computer loads Windows and displays the Program Manager. Locate the Lotus Applications program group icon, probably at the bottom of your screen, as shown in Figure 2-3.

3 Double-click the Lotus Applications group icon
The Lotus Applications group window opens and the Lotus 1-2-3 Release 4 icon displays, as shown in Figure 2-4. Your screen might look different depending on which applications are installed on your computer.

4 Double-click the Lotus 1-2-3 Release 4 icon
Lotus 1-2-3 opens and displays an untitled worksheet. Turn to the next lesson, "Viewing the Lotus 1-2-3 screen" to see a new, Untitled worksheet.

FIGURE 2-3: Lotus Applications group icon in Program Manager

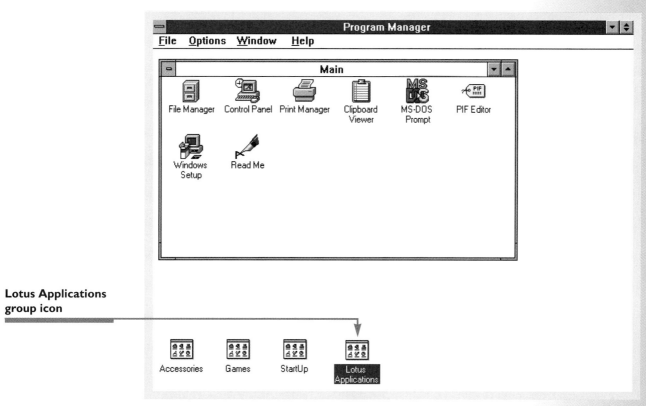

Lotus Applications
group icon

FIGURE 2-4: Lotus 1-2-3 Release 4 program icon

Lotus 1-2-3 Release 4
icon

Lotus Applications
window

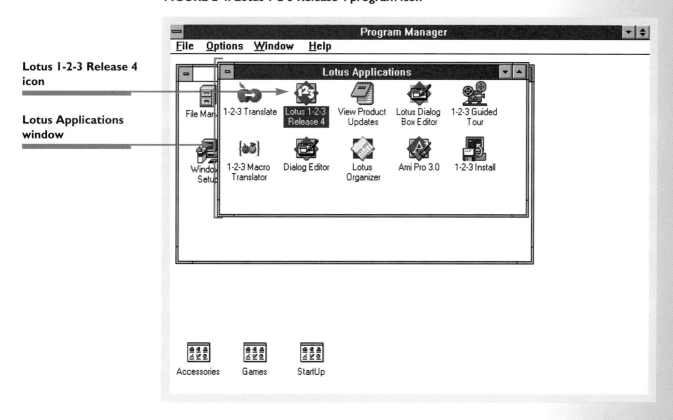

Viewing the Lotus 1-2-3 screen

When you start Lotus 1-2-3, the computer displays both the **worksheet window**, the gridded area where you enter data, and Lotus 1-2-3 **screen elements**. The screen elements enable you to create and work with worksheets. Familiarize yourself with the Lotus 1-2-3 worksheet window and screen elements by comparing the descriptions below to Figure 2-5.

▪ The **worksheet window** contains a grid of columns and rows. Columns are labeled alphabetically (A,B,C, etc.) and rows are labeled numerically (1,2,3 etc.) The worksheet window only displays a tiny fraction of the whole worksheet, which has a total of 256 columns and 8,192 rows. The intersection of a column and a row is a **cell**. Every cell has its own unique location or **cell address**, which is identified by the coordinates of the intersecting column and row. For example, the cell address of the first cell on a worksheet is A1.

▪ The **cell pointer** is a dark border that highlights the cell you are working on, or the **current cell**. In Figure 2-5, the cell pointer is located at A1, so A1 is the current cell. To make another cell current, click any other cell or press the direction keys on your keyboard.

▪ The **title bar** displays the application name (Lotus 1-2-3 Release 4) and the filename of the open worksheet (in this case, 'Untitled'). The title bar also contains a control menu box and resizing buttons, which you learned about in Unit 1.

▪ The **main menu bar** contains pull-down menus from which you choose Lotus 1-2-3 commands.

▪ The **edit line** displays information about the current cell, and provides tools for entering data into the worksheet. At the far left of the edit line is the **selection indicator**, which displays the cell address of the current cell. In Figure 2-5, A1 displays in the selection indicator, which means that A1 is the current cell.

▪ **SmartIcons** are tools that give you easy access to a variety of commonly used Lotus 1-2-3 commands. To choose a SmartIcon command, simply click it with the left mouse button. SmartIcons show graphic representations of commands. For instance, the SmartIcon for printing depicts a miniature printer.

▪ The **status bar** at the bottom of the screen displays information about the active cell, and also provides tools for formatting. At the far right is the **mode indicator**, which informs you of the Lotus 1-2-3's status.

FIGURE 2-5: Lotus 1-2-3 screen elements and worksheet window

Title bar

Main menu bar

Edit line

SmartIcons

Current cell

Cell pointer

Worksheet window

Status bar

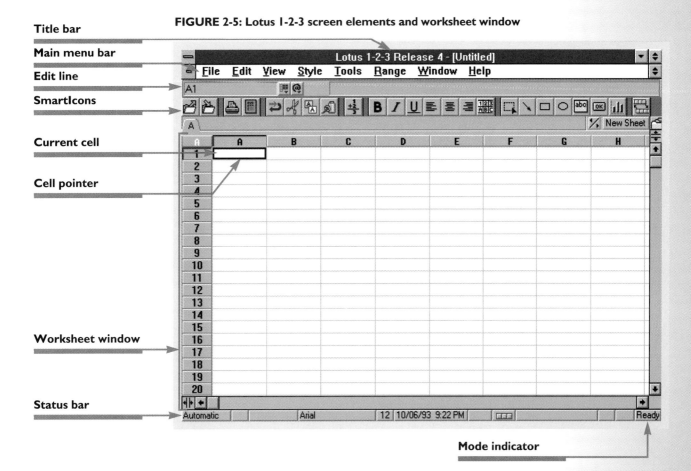

Mode indicator

Compatibility with the Classic window

The Lotus 1-2-3 Classic window allows you to use the menu from version 3.1 of
Lotus 1-2-3. To access this menu, press **[/]** or **[<]** when the mode indicator displays **Ready**. When you complete a command or press **[Esc]**, the program
returns to the regular menu. You cannot use the mouse when working in the
Classic window.

TROUBLE?

If your worksheet
does not fill the
screen as shown in
Figure 2-5, click the
maximize button.■

Working with menus and dialog boxes

Like many other Windows applications, you choose most commands in Lotus 1-2-3 using menus. When you choose a command that is followed by an ellipsis (...) a dialog box displays. A **dialog box** is a window which requires you to choose specific options before the command can be executed. Table 2-1 describes how to choose some of the most common dialog box options. ▶ Try using menu and dialog box commands to enter the title for Lucinda Riley's budget worksheet that you saw in Figure 2-2, earlier in this unit.

1   Click cell **A1** to make it the current cell
The cell pointer surrounds A1, and the selection box indicator displays 'A1.'

2   Type **Budget** then press **[Enter]**
The word Budget displays in cell A1. Notice that the word Budget is aligned on the left side of the cell. To center it in the cell, you will use a command from the Style menu.

3   Click **Style** on the menu bar to open the Style menu
The Style menu opens, as shown in Figure 2-6, displaying a list of commands relating to the appearance of the worksheet.

4   Click **Alignment**
The Alignment dialog box displays, presenting you with many options for changing the appearance of the current cell. See Figure 2-7.

5   In the Horizontal option box, click the round circle next to the word **Center**
The round circle is called a **radio button**. Radio buttons display when only one option can be chosen in a dialog box.

6   Click OK
The dialog box closes and the word Budget is now centered in cell A1.

TABLE 2-1:
Common dialog box options

DIALOG BOX ELEMENT	EXAMPLE	DESCRIPTION/HOW TO USE
check box	☒ Wrap text	a square box that you click to turn an option on or off.
text box	tours.wk4	a box in which you type text
radio button	⦿ Center	a small circle that you click to choose a single option
command button	OK	a button you click to carry out a command
list box	▤ c: ms-dos_5 ⯆	a box containing a list of items. To choose an item, click the down scroll arrow, then click the desired item.

FIGURE 2-6: Worksheet with Style menu open

Ellipsis (...) indicates a dialog box will display

Open style menu

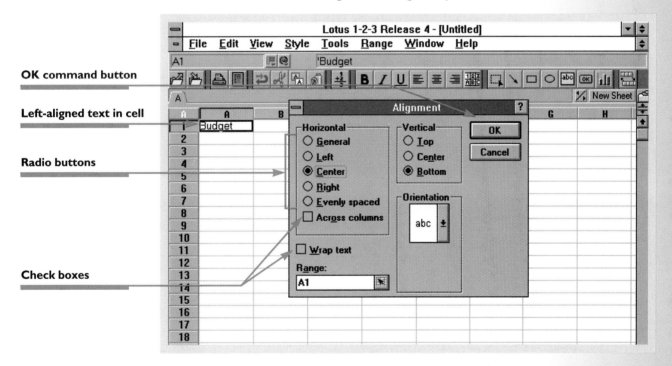

FIGURE 2-7: Worksheet with Alignment dialog box open

OK command button

Left-aligned text in cell

Radio buttons

Check boxes

Using keyboard shortcuts

Cursor or direction keys can be used to make choices within a dialog box or menu. To choose a menu from the keyboard, press **[F10]** and use **[→]** or **[←]** to select a menu. To choose a command from a menu, use **[↓]** or **[↑]**, then press **[Enter]** to make your selection.

QUICK **TIP**

To close a menu without choosing a command, click anywhere outside the menu, or press **[Esc]**.∎

Working with SmartIcons

SmartIcons are tools that give you easy access to a variety of commonly used Lotus 1-2-3 commands. Clicking a SmartIcon to execute a command offers a faster alternative to clicking open a menu and then clicking a command. SmartIcons are organized in a **palette**, as shown in Figure 2-8. This is the default SmartIcon palette that is in place when you first install Lotus 1-2-3, but there are also other ready-made or **predefined** SmartIcon palettes you can use if you prefer. Try using the bold SmartIcon to format your worksheet title, then explore some of the other SmartIcon palettes. See Table 2-2 for a description of the most common SmartIcons.

1   Click cell **A1** to make it the current cell, then click the **Bold SmartIcon** 🅱
The word Budget becomes bold. The bold SmartIcon is a **toggle button,** which means that if you clicked the bold SmartIcon again, you would remove the bold formatting. Try viewing other SmartIcon palettes.

2   Click the **SmartIcon selector button** ▦ at the bottom of your screen
A pop-up menu displays a list of other predefined SmartIcon palettes. See Figure 2-9.

3   Watch the SmartIcon palette, then click **Editing** from the list
The SmartIcon palette changes to display SmartIcons relating to editing. Take a look at the other available SmartIcon palettes by first clicking the SmartIcon selector button and then clicking each palette name from the popup list. Do not click Hide SmartIcons. When you have viewed them all, continue to step 4.

4   Click ▦, then click **Default Sheet**
The Default SmartIcon palette displays. We will use this SmartIcon palette throughout this book except when otherwise noted.

TABLE 2-2:
Common SmartIcons

ICON	NAME	DESCRIPTION
📂	Open	Opens a file
💾	Save	Saves a file
🖨	Print	Opens the Print dialog box
✂	Cut	Cuts the selected area to the Clipboard
📋	Copy	Copies the selected area to the Clipboard
📄	Paste	Pastes Clipboard contents
B	Bold	Adds/removes bold formatting
▤	Align left	Aligns cell contents to the left

FIGURE 2-8: Default SmartIcon palette

Bold SmartIcon

Default SmartIcon
palette

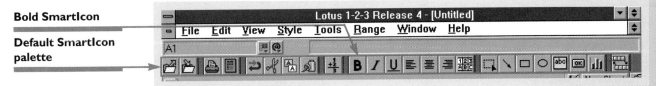

FIGURE 2-9: Worksheet with SmartIcon selector button

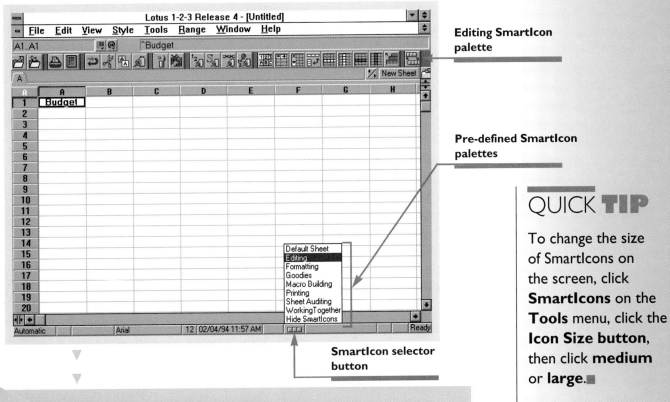

Editing SmartIcon
palette

Pre-defined SmartIcon
palettes

SmartIcon selector
button

Repositioning SmartIcons

You can change the location of SmartIcons on
the screen. This can help you make the best use
of the monitor. To change the locations, choose
SmartIcons from the **Tools** menu, click the
down arrow in the Position list box. Choose where
you want to locate the SmartIcons: Floating, Left,
Top, Right, or Bottom and click OK. A worksheet
showing repositioned SmartIcons and another
palette of SmartIcons is shown in Figure 2-11.

SmartIcons to be used
with Chart command

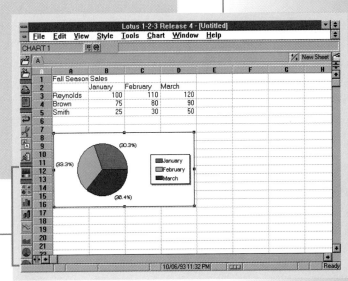

FIGURE 2-10: Chart-related SmartIcons on left side of screen

Getting Help

Lotus 1-2-3 features an extensive on-line Help utility which gives you immmediate access to definitions, explanations, and useful tips. Help information displays in a separate window that you can resize and refer to as you work. ► Lucinda decides to use Help to learn about SmartIcons.

1 Click **Help** on the menu bar, then click **Search**
The Search dialog box opens, as shown in Figure 2-11. You use this dialog box to look up a specific topic or feature.

2 In the Search dialog text box, type **SmartIcons**
Notice that topic 'SmartIcons' appears in the list box below the text box.

3 Click the **Show topics button**, then click **SmartIcons, Defined** in the topics list

4 Click the **Go To button**
A Help window opens, displaying a definition of SmartIcons and some basic information on how to use them. Lucinda reads this, then decides to use the How Do I feature to get information on how to use SmartIcons.

5 Click the **Contents button** on the Help button bar
The Help contents window opens, listing available Help topics as shown in Figure 2-12. The green underlined items indicate a cross reference to a Help topic.

6 Move the mouse pointer over **How Do I?** in the list of underlined topics and **click** when the pointer turns to a 🖑
The How Do I window opens, listing topics that teach you how to do specific tasks.

7 Click the topic **Use SmartIcons**
A new window opens, displaying information about how to use SmartIcons. Page through the document using the Help buttons described in Table 2-3.

8 Click **File** in the Help window menu bar, then click **Exit**
The Help utility closes and you return to your worksheet.

TABLE 2-3:
The Help buttons

BUTTON	DESCRIPTION
Contents	Displays the contents of the Help file by subject grouping
Search	Provides a dialog box where you can type the word or command you want help with
Back	Returns you to the previous topic
History	Shows you a list of Help topics that you have recently referred to
<<	Moves to the previous page
>>	Moves to the next page

FIGURE 2-11: Search dialog box

Type desired topic in
text box

Go To button

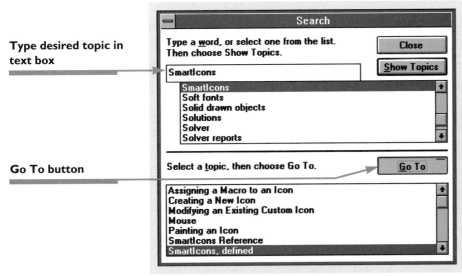

QUICK **TIP**

To get help with what
you are doing, point
to a command on a
menu or a part of the
worksheet and press
[F1]. Help displays
information about
where you are in
Lotus 1-2-3.■

FIGURE 2-12: Help Contents window

Contents button

Contents, click a
listing to get help

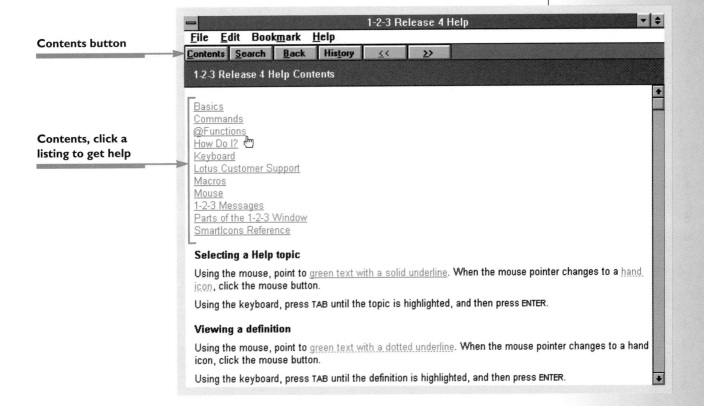

Moving around the worksheet

With more than two million cells available to you in a Lotus 1-2-3 worksheet, it's important to know how to navigate. There are many methods for moving around. If you simply want to move up, down, or over one or two cells, an easy method is to press the direction keys ([↑] [↓] [→] [←]). For longer distances, you might prefer to use the mouse, by clicking the desired cell address. If your desired cell address is not visible within the worksheet window, then you can use the scroll bars or the Go To command to move the location into view. Table 2-4 lists helpful shortcuts for moving around the Lotus 1-2-3 worksheet. Try navigating the worksheet now using a combination of these different methods.

1 **Click cell H20**
The cell pointer highlights cell H20, in the lower right corner of your worksheet window.

2 **Press [→]**
The cell pointer moves over one cell to I20, moving the entire worksheet over one column. Notice that A1, which contains the title 'Budget' is no longer visible in the worksheet window.

3 **On the vertical scroll bar, click the down arrow once**
The worksheet window scrolls down one row, so that row 21 moves into view. You can move a window's contents in small increments by clicking on the vertical scroll bar arrows. You can move up or down by a whole screenful at a time by clicking on either side of a scroll box.

4 **Click to the right of the horizontal scroll box**
The cell in in the lower right corner of the screen should be Q21. If you need to travel a great distance across a worksheet, you can use the Go To command.

5 **Press [F5] located in the function keys area of your keyboard**
The Go To dialog box displays.

6 **Type Z1000 in the textbox, as shown in Figure 2-13, and click OK**
The cell pointer now highlights cell Z1000 in the upper left corner of the screen. You could use the Go To command or scroll bars to get you back to the beginning of the worksheet, but there is a faster method which moves the cell pointer directly to A1.

7 **Press [Home]**
The cell pointer now highlights cell A1, and you are back at the beginning of your worksheet.

FIGURE 2-13: The worksheet with the Go To dialog box open

Vertical scroll box

Type desired cell address in text box

Vertical scroll bar

Horizontal scroll box

Horizontal scroll bar

TABLE 2-4: Getting around the worksheet

TO MOVE	DO THIS
Up a row	Press [↑]
Cell left	Press [←]
Cell right	Press [→]
Down a row	Press [↓]
To a specific cell	Press [F5] and Enter cell address or range
Column left	Click the left arrow on the horizontal scroll bar
Column right	Click the right arrow on the horizontal scroll bar

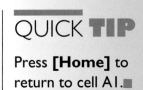

QUICK **TIP**

Press **[Home]** to return to cell A1.■

Closing a file and exiting Lotus 1-2-3

When you have finished working on a worksheet, save the file and close it. To close a file, click **Close** on the File menu as shown in Figure 2-14. ▶ When you have completed all your work on Lotus 1-2-3, you need to exit the application. To exit Lotus 1-2-3, click **Exit** on the File menu. For a comparison of these two tasks refer to Table 2-5.

1 Click **File** in the main menu bar, then click **Close**
Figure 2-14 shows the File menu. The Close dialog box displays, asking if you want to save changes before closing. See Figure 2-15. Because this was only a practice session, there is no need to save the file.

2 Click No

3 Click **File**, then click **Exit**
Lotus 1-2-3 closes and frees up computer memory for other computing tasks. If you are ending your session now, continue to step 4.

4 Click **File** on the Program Manager menu bar, then click **Exit Windows**
A dialog box displays.

5 Click **OK**
Windows closes and the DOS command prompt displays.

TABLE 2-5:
Understanding the Close and Exit commands

CLOSING A FILE	EXITING LOTUS 1-2-3
Puts a file away	Puts *all* open files away
Leaves Lotus 1-2-3 loaded in computer memory	Frees computer memory up for other uses

FIGURE 2-14: Closing a worksheet using the File menu

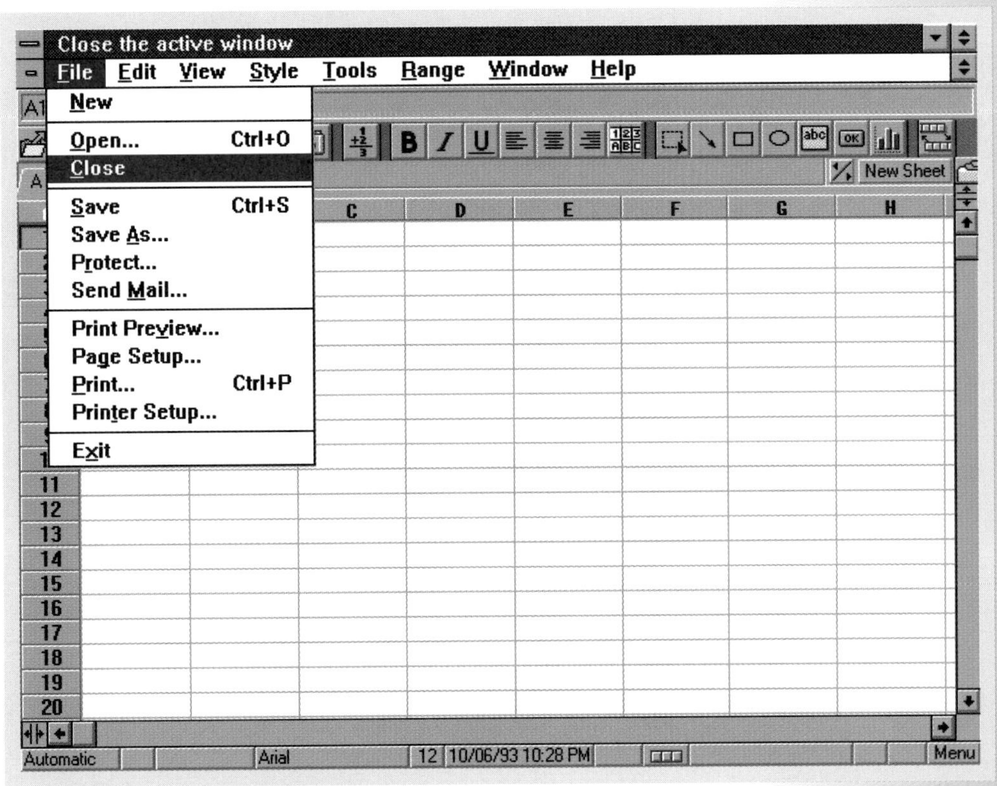

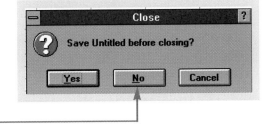

FIGURE 2-15: The Close dialog box

Click No to discard document

QUICK **TIP**

To exit Lotus 1-2-3 and close several files at once, choose **Exit** from the File menu. Lotus 1-2-3 prompts you to save changes to each worksheet.■

CONCEPTSREVIEW

Label each of the elements of the Lotus 1-2-3 screen shown in Figure 2-16.

1 _____

2 _____

3 _____

4 _____

5 _____

6 _____

7 _____

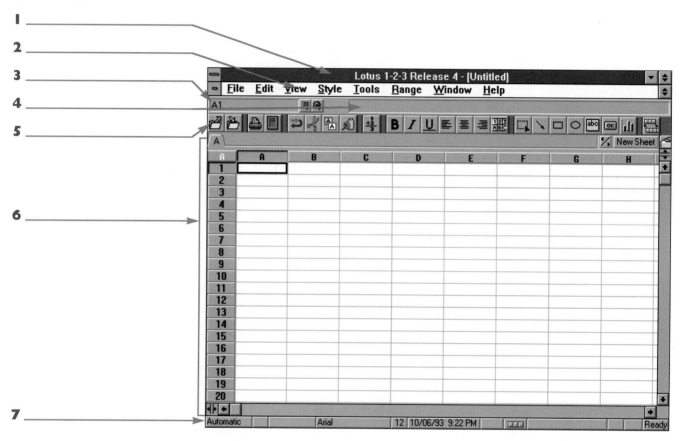

FIGURE 2-16

Match each of the terms with the statement that describes its function.

8 Document that contains a grid of columns and rows

9 The intersection of a column and row

10 Graphic symbol that depicts a task or function

11 Area that displays the worksheet name

12 Rectangle that indicates the worksheet cell you are currently working in

a. Cell pointer

b. SmartIcon

c. Worksheet

d. Cell

e. Title bar

Select the best answer from the list of choices.

13 An electronic spreadsheet can perform all of the following tasks, EXCEPT:

a. Displaying information visually

b. Calculating data accurately

c. Planning worksheet goals

d. Recalculating updated information

14 The term for moving different sections of the worksheet into view is:

a. Searching

b. Scrolling

c. Selecting

d. Shifting

15 Which key do you press to move quickly to cell A1?

a. [Home]

b. [Alt]

c. [Esc]

d. [Enter]

16 A menu command that is followed by an ellipsis means that:

a. The command is not currently available

b. Clicking the command will open a dialog box

c. Clicking the command will open a submenu

d. The command has no keyboard shortcut

17 You can get Lotus 1-2-3 Help any of the following ways, EXCEPT:

a. Clicking Help on the main menu bar

b. Pressing the [F1] key

c. Selecting a topic in the Help window

d. Minimizing the application window

18 Which key(s) do you press to move the worksheet right by one column?

a. [Enter]

b. [→]

c. [Esc]

d. [Alt][R]

APPLICATIONSREVIEW

1 Launch Lotus 1-2-3 and identify items on the worksheet.

a. Turn on the computer if necessary.

b. At the DOS prompt, type WIN then press [Enter].

c. Double-click the Lotus Applications group icon if the window is not open.

d. Double-click the Lotus 1-2-3 icon. After the application loads, the default worksheet displays.

e. Try to identify as many items on the worksheet as you can, without referring to the lesson material.

2 Explore Lotus 1-2-3 menus.

a. Click Edit on the menu bar.

b. Point at the Undo command, but do not let go of the mouse button. Notice that a description of the highlighted Undo command appears in the title bar.

c. Continue pointing at commands on the Edit menu so that you can review brief descriptions in the title bar. Notice that several of the Edit commands are followed by elipses (...). This means the command opens a dialog box, which lets you provide additional information.

d. Now click Tools on the menu bar.

e. Drag through the commands and review the descriptions in the title bar. Notice that several of the Tools commands are followed by arrows. The arrow indicates that the command leads to a cascade menu.

f. Click the Draw command. The cascade menu displays as shown in Figure 2-17.

g. Continue reviewing other commands on the Lotus 1-2-3 menu bar in the same fashion.

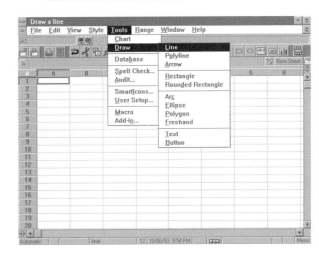

3 Practice moving the cell pointer in the worksheet.

   a. Press [Home]. The cell pointer moves to the upper-left corner of the worksheet. This is cell A1, as shown in the selection indicator.

   b. Press [→] once to move the cell pointer right one column. The selection indicator displays B1.

   c. Press [↓] twice. Watch the cell pointer move down two rows to cell B3.

   d. Click the right arrow on the horizontal scroll bar. Notice that the screen shifts the column display to the right by one column.

   e. Now click the left arrow on the horizontal scroll bar. The screen shifts back to its original column display.

4 Explore Lotus 1-2-3 Help in the worksheet.

   a. Click Help on the menu bar from the default 1-2-3 worksheet and view the Help commands.

   b. Click Search. The Search dialog box displays.

   c. Try to identify all of the buttons that appear in the Search dialog box, as shown in Figure 2-18.

   d. Click the down arrow on the topic list box scroll bar to view available topics.

   e. Select a word from the list box, then click the Show Topics button. Help displays the various topics related to the selection.

   f. Select a topic to read, then click the Go To button.

   g. Click File on the Help menu bar then click Exit..

5 Practice minimizing and restoring the worksheet window.

   a. Click the minimize button in the Untitled worksheet. The worksheet window minimizes to an icon on the screen.

   b. Double-click the untitled worksheet icon to restore it to its original size.

6 Close the worksheet and exit Lotus 1-2-3.

   a. Click File on the menu bar then click Close. The dialog box asks if you want to save any changes. You do not want to save this worksheet file.

   b. Click No. The dialog box closes.

   c. If needed, close any other worksheets you may have opened. Follow the steps above to do so.

   d. Click File on the menu bar then click Exit. Lotus 1-2-3 closes.

INDEPENDENT
REVIEW

Lotus 1-2-3 provides an online Guided Tour that gives you a quick overview of the graphic worksheet window. The Guided Tour covers elements such as the cell pointer, status bar, and SmartIcons. The Guided Tour also covers how to use online Help to get detailed information about Lotus 1-2-3 commands and options.

Ask your instructor how to access the Lotus 1-2-3 Guided Tour or the online Tutorial.

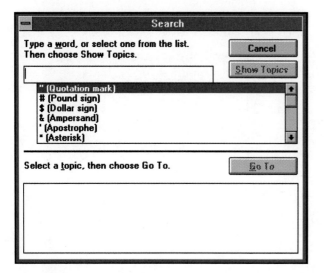

FIGURE 2-18

UNIT 3

OBJECTIVES

▶ Plan and design a worksheet

▶ Enter labels

▶ Enter values

▶ Edit cell entries

▶ Enter formulas

▶ Use Lotus 1-2-3 functions

▶ Save a worksheet

▶ Print a worksheet

Building
A WORKSHEET

ow that you are familiar with menus, dialog boxes, SmartIcons, and the Help window and know how to navigate within a Lotus 1-2-3 worksheet, you are ready to plan and build your own worksheet. When you build a worksheet, you enter text, values, and formulas into worksheet cells. Once you create a worksheet, you can save and print it. ▶ Helping managers plan for the future is one of the many ways Lotus 1-2-3 is useful for businesses. Pat Anderson, the owner of the All Outdoors Tour and Travel Company, wants to forecast this year's anticipated summer business volume by using last year's figures. ▶

Planning and designing a worksheet

Before you enter data into a worksheet, you need to plan what you want your worksheet to accomplish and how you want it to look. At the All Outdoors Company, Pat Anderson needs to plan a worksheet that will report 1994 summer tour sales, and forecast summer tour sales for 1995. Pat's 1995 sales goal is to increase the 1994 sales totals by 20 percent. Using Figure 3-1 and the planning guidelines below, follow Pat as she sketches out her worksheet plan.

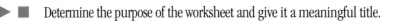

■ Determine the purpose of the worksheet and give it a meaningful title.

Pat needs to report summer tour sales data for 1994 and then forecast summer tour sales for 1995. Pat titles the worksheet "1994 Summer Tour Sales with Forecast for 1995"

■ Determine the results you want to get from your worksheet. Any results you get from your worksheet is called **output**.

Pat needs to determine what the 1995 sales totals would be if sales increased by 20% over the total 1994 summer tour sales.

■ Collect all the information that will produce the results you want to see. This information that you enter into the worksheet is called **input**.

Pat gathers together all her sales data for the 1994 summer tour season. The summer season runs from June through August. The types of tours sold in these months include Bike, Raft, Horse, and Bus.

■ Determine the calculations you need to put in your worksheet to get the results you want. These calculations are called **formulas**.

Pat first needs to total the number of tours sold for each month of the 1994 season. Then she needs to add all the monthly totals together to determine a grand total of 1994 summer tour sales. Finally, Pat needs to multiply the 1994 totals by 1.2 to calculate a 20% increase for 1995.

■ Roughly sketch on paper how the worksheet will look. Use this sketch to decide where to place labels, data, and calculations.

*Pat decides to put tour types in the rows, and the months in the columns. These text entries which describe the data in the worksheet are called **labels**. Labels help you understand the information in a worksheet. Next, Pat enters the tour sales data in her sketch. These are called **values**. Values are used in calculations. Pat indicates where the totals for all monthly sales should go. Below the totals, she writes out a formula for determining a 20% increase in sales for 1995.*

FIGURE 3-1: Worksheet sketch showing labels, values, and calculations

1994 Summer Tour Sales with Forecast for 1995

	June	July	August	Totals
Bike	14	10	6	3 month total
Raft	7	8	12	
Horse	12	7	6	
Bus	1	2	9	↓
Totals	June Total	July Total	August Total	Grand Total for 1994
1995 Sales	Total x 1.2	———————————————→		

Entering labels

Labels are used to identify the data in the rows and columns of a worksheet, and are also used to make your worksheet understandable. For this reason, you should enter all labels in your worksheet first. Labels usually contain text, but can also contain numerical information such as dates, times, or address numbers that are not used in calculations. ▶ Using Pat's sketch as a guide, start building her worksheet by entering the labels.

1   In the Untitled worksheet on your screen, click cell **B4** to make it the current cell
    Notice that the cell address, B4, displays in the selection indicator in the edit line. Now enter the worksheet title.

2   Type **1994 Summer Tour Sales with Forecast for 1995** then press **[Enter]**
    Pressing **[Enter]** confirms your entry. Notice that the full title displays on the screen, even though it is longer that the current cell. For all labels, Lotus 1-2-3 displays the remaining characters in the next cell as long as it is empty. Look at the Contents box in the edit line and notice that there is an apostrophe before '1994.' The apostrophe is called a **label prefix**. Anytime your cell entry contains text, Lotus 1-2-3 recognizes the entry as a label and inserts this apostrophe prefix, which automatically aligns the label on the left side of the cell. See Table 3-1 for other label prefixes. Now enter the labels for the summer month sales into the columns of the worksheet.

3   Click cell **B5** and type **"June**, then press **[Enter]**
    Because you entered the quotes prefix, the entry is right-aligned.

4   Press **[→]** to make C5 the current cell then type **"July**; click **D5** then type **"August**; click **E5** then type **"Total** then press **[Enter]**
    Pressing one of the direction keys to move to another cell is another way to confirm an entry. Now enter the labels for the rows, starting with the tour types.

5   Click cell **A6** then type **Bike**; click cell **A7** then type **Raft**, click cell **A8** then type **Horse**; click cell **A9** then type **Bus** then press **[Enter]**
    Now enter the labels for the rows containing the totals and the 1995 sales forecast.

6   Click cell **A11** then type **Total**, click cell **A13** then type **1995 Sales**, then press **[Enter]**
    All labels for Pat's worksheet should be entered. Check your work against Figure 3-2.

TABLE 3-1:
Label prefixes

LABEL PREFIX	ALIGNMENT	EXAMPLE
'	Aligns at left side of cell	Tour Type
"	Aligns at right side of cell	June
^	Aligns at center of cell	Pat

FIGURE 3-2: Worksheet with labels

Selection indicator

Contents Box shows
label prefix

Row labels

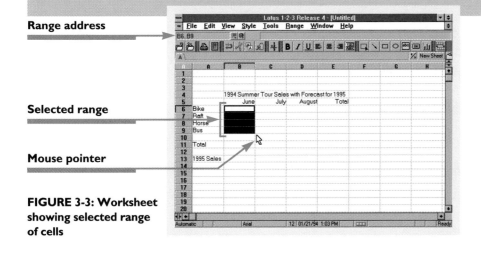

Selecting a range of cells

To enter data in a particular cell, you must first click the cell where you want the data to go. Clicking a cell is called **selecting** the cell. Often it's useful to select more than one cell. Any group of cells (two or more) is called a **range**. To select a range using the mouse, click the first cell and drag to the last cell you want included in the range. To select a range using the keyboard, place the cell pointer on the first cell in the range, and while pressing **[Shift]**, move the pointer to the last cell, using the arrow keys. Figure 3-3 shows a selected range. Notice that the range address in the selection indicator shows the first and last cells in the range (B6..B9). In the next lesson, you practice entering values into a selected range.

Range address

Selected range

Mouse pointer

FIGURE 3-3: Worksheet showing selected range of cells

TROUBLE?

All lessons from this point on assume you have Lotus 1-2-3 running. If you need help with this, go back to the lesson called "Starting Lotus 1-2-3" for Windows in Unit 2.■

Entering Values

Values, which can include numbers, formulas, and functions, are used in calculations. Lotus 1-2-3 recognizes an entry as a value when it begins with a number or any of these symbols: +,–,=,@, #, or $. All values are right-aligned by default. Whenever you enter a value in a cell, the word 'Value' displays in the Mode indicator located on the far right of the status bar. Refer to Table 3-2 for more information on the Mode indicator. ▶ Try entering sales data from the 1994 summer tour season into Pat's worksheet.

1 Click cell **B6**, type **14**, then press **[Enter]**
You entered the June bike tour information and confirmed the entry by pressing **[Enter]**. Continue entering the June sales data for the other tour types.

2 Click cell **B7** and type **7**; click cell **B8** then type **12**; click cell **B9** then type **1**
All the tour sales for the month of June are now entered. This time, you confirmed each entry by clicking on a new cell. Now try entering the July sales figures by first selecting a range, and then entering your data.

3 Click cell **C6** and drag to cell **C9** to select the range **C6..C9**
Notice when you drag to select the range that the pointer shape changes to a 🖑. All the data cells for the month of July are selected, and the cell pointer is on cell C6 . Now enter the number of July bike tours.

4 Type **10** then press **[Enter]**
The pointer moves to the next cell in the range, which is C7, the raft tour sales. Continue entering the sales figures in the rest of the selected range (cells C7, C8, and C9) by following the instructions in step 5.

5 Type **8** in **C7** then press **[Enter]**; type **7** in **C8** then press **[Enter]**; type **2** in **C9** then press **[Enter]**
You have entered all the July sales. Try filling in the August column using the same method.

6 Click cell **D6** and drag to cell **D9** to select the range **D6..D9**
Again the pointer shape changes to a 🖑. All the data cells for the month of August are selected. D6 is the current cell.

7 Type **6** in **D6** then press **[Enter]**; type **12** in **D7** then press **[Enter]**; type **6** in **D8** then press **[Enter]**; type **9** in **D9** then press **[Enter]**
Cells D6 through D9 now contain all the August tour sales data. Compare your worksheet to Figure 3-4.

FIGURE 3-4: Worksheet with labels and values entered

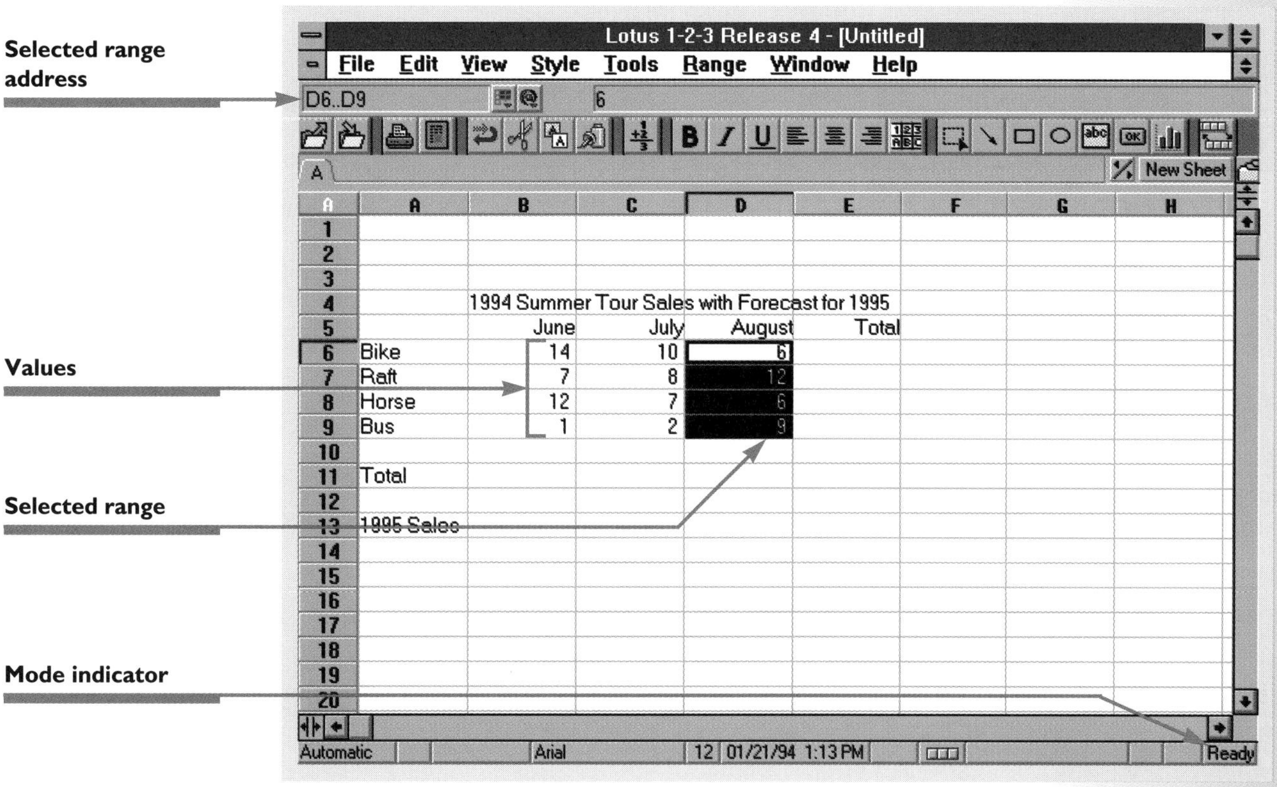

Selected range address

Values

Selected range

Mode indicator

TABLE 3-2: Understanding the mode indicator

MODE INDICATOR	DESCRIPTION
Edit	You are entering, editing, or have made an incorrect entry
Error	You have made an entry Lotus can not understand; choose Help **[F1]** or click **OK**
Label	You are typing a label
Menu	You have clicked the Menu bar at the top of the screen
Point	You have specified a range without a formula
Ready	Lotus 1-2-3 is ready for you to enter data or choose a command
Value	You are entering a value that can be used in calculations
Wait	Lotus 1-2-3 is completing a task

TROUBLE?

Labels or values can be edited after they have been confirmed. Select the cell you want to edit and press **[F2]**. Then use the Backspace and Delete keys to make any corrections. Press **[Enter]** to confirm, or simply move the pointer to another cell.■

Editing cell entries

In Lotus 1-2-3, you can change the contents of any cell whether it contains labels or values at any time. To edit the contents of a cell, you first select the cell you want to edit, and then put Lotus 1-2-3 into Edit mode by either clicking the Contents box, pressing [F2], or double clicking the selected cell. To make sure you are in Edit mode, check the mode indicator. Table 3-3 lists some common editing keys. ▶ After checking her worksheet, Pat discovers that she needs to change the value for June bus tours. She also decides to add canoe sales data to the raft sales figures.

1 Click cell **B9**

This selects the number of June bus tours. Pat needs to change this value to 2.

2 Click anywhere in the Contents box

The Contents box is shown in Figure 3-5. Lotus 1-2-3 goes into Edit mode, and the Mode indicator displays 'Edit.'

3 Press **[Backspace]**, type **2** then press **[Enter]**

Instead of pressing **[Enter]** to confirm your entry, you could also click the check mark to the left of the Contents box. See "Using the Cancel and Confirm buttons" on the opposite page for more information.

Pat now needs to add '/Canoe' to the Raft label.

4 Click cell **A7**, then press **[F2]**

Lotus 1-2-3 is in Edit mode again.

5 Type **/Canoe** then press **[Enter]**

The label changes to **Raft/Canoe**.

6 Double click cell **B7**

Double clicking a cell also puts Lotus 1-2-3 into Edit mode.

7 Press **[Backspace]**, type **9**, then press **[Enter]**

See Figure 3-5. Lotus 1-2-3 enters the new value and leaves Edit mode.

TABLE 3-3:
Lotus 1-2-3 common editing keys

KEY	FUNCTION
F2	Changes the mode indicator to Edit and displays the selected cell contents in the Contents box
Backspace	Removes highlighted text immediately to the left of the insertion point
Del	Removes highlighted text immediately to the right of the insertion point

FIGURE 3-5: Worksheet in Edit mode

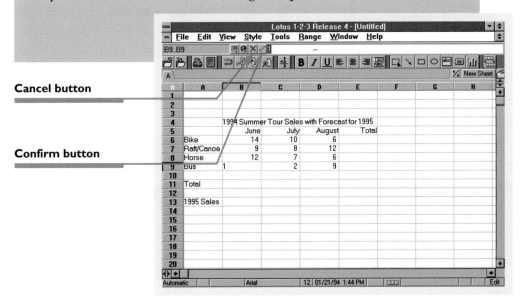

Contents box

Cell in Edit mode

Mode indicator

Using the Cancel and Confirm buttons

When entering data into a cell, the edit line at the top of the screen displays the **Confirm button** (a check mark) and the **Cancel button** (an X), as shown in Figure 3-6. Confirm an entry by clicking the Confirm button. Clicking the Cancel button removes the data entered and leaves a blank cell or the previous entry. These buttons are useful when editing a complex formula in the Contents box.

Cancel button

Confirm button

FIGURE 3-6: Cancel and Confirm buttons

QUICK

If you make a mistake, choose **Undo** from the Edit menu or click the **Undo SmartIcon** before doing anything else.■

Entering formulas

Formulas are used to perform numeric calculations such as adding, multiplying and averaging. All formulas use special symbols called mathematical **operators** to perform calculations. See Table 3-4 for a list of Lotus 1-2-3 operators. Because it is useful to perform calculations by referring to a particular cell or range, formulas often contain cell addresses. Using a cell address in a formula is called **cell referencing**. Using cell references keeps your worksheet up-to-date and accurate. If you change a value in a cell, any formula containing that cell reference will automatically recalculate using the new value. ▶ Now, use formulas to add the total tours for June, July, and August in Pat's worksheet.

STEPS

1 Click cell **B11**
This is the cell where Pat wants to put the calculation for total June sales.

2 Type **+** (plus sign)
The plus operator at the beginning of an entry tells Lotus 1-2-3 that a formula is about to be entered, and the first value is positive. Now Pat is going to enter a formula for calculating the total June sales. She will use cell references.

3 Type **b6+b7+b8+b9** then press **[Enter]**
The result of 37 is shown in the cell, and the formula for cell B11 is displayed in the Contents box. Next, add the numbers of tours in the July column.

4 Click cell **C11** and type **+c6+c7+c8+c9** then press **[Enter]**
The result of 27 is shown in C11. Finally, enter the formula to calculate the August tour sales.

5 Click cell **D11**, then type **+d6+d7+d8+d9** then press **[Enter]**
The total tour sales for August display in cell D11. Compare your results with Figure 3-7.

TABLE 3-4:
Lotus 1-2-3 mathematical operators

OPERATOR	PURPOSE	EXAMPLE
+	Performs addition	+A1+A2
–	Performs subtraction	+A2-10
*	Performs multiplication	+A1*A4
/	Performs division	+A3/A6

FIGURE 3-7: Worksheet showing formula and result

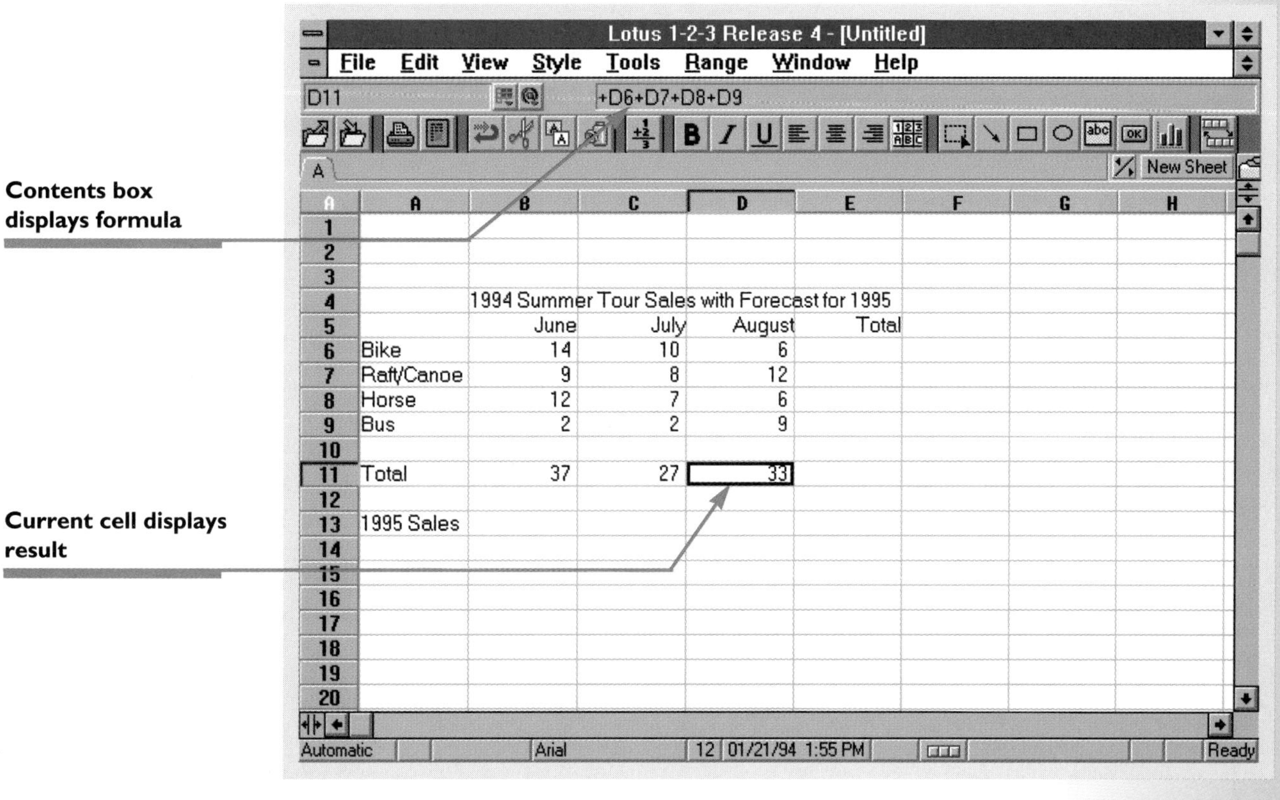

Contents box
displays formula

Current cell displays
result

Understanding cell referencing

When you create a formula, you can either type a value or use **cell referencing**.
Cell referencing, or including a cell address in a formula, helps prevent typographical
errors and makes it easy to update formulas. When including a cell reference, you
can either type the cell address (for example, A1) or click the desired cell. To insert
a range of cells in a formula, click the first cell and drag to the last cell of the range.

TROUBLE?

If the formula instead
of the result displays in
the cell after you press
[Enter], check that
you began the formula
with a + (plus sign).■

Entering formulas, continued

Now that Pat has calculated the total tour sales for 1994, she can use these figures to calculate her forecast for 1995. She will use the multiplication symbol, * (the asterisk), to write the formula calculating a 20% increase of 1994 sales.

6 Click cell **B13**, type **+b11*1.2** then press **[Enter]**
This formula, which displays in the Contents box, calculates the result of multiplying cell B11 by 1.2. The result of 44.4 displays in cell B13. Now calculate a 20% increase for the July column.

7 Click cell **C13**, type **+c11*1.2** then press **[Enter]**
The result of 32.4 displays in cell C13. Now calculate a 20% increase for the August column. This time, instead of typing in the cell reference, try clicking the cell address.

8 Click cell **D13**, type **+**, click cell **D11**, type *, type **1.2** then press **[Enter]**
The result of 39.6 displays in D13, and the formula displays in the Contents box. Compare your results with Figure 3-8.

FIGURE 3-8: Worksheet showing formula and result for 20% increase

Contents box displays formula for 20% increase

Cell displays result of formula

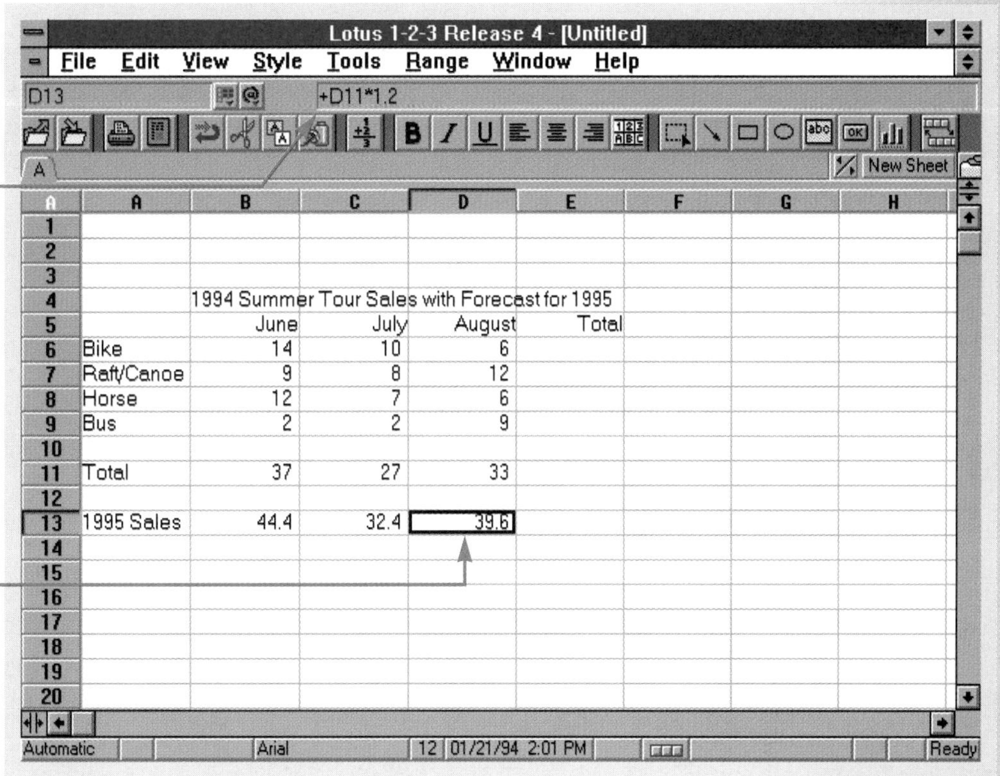

How Lotus 1-2-3 calculates a formula

The formulas for Pat's calculations involve only one math operator—multiplication. But a formula may include several calculations. When you work with formulas that have more than one operator, the **order of operations** is very important.

If a formula contains two or more operators, such as $4 + .55/4000$, the computer performs the calculations in a particular sequence, based on these rules:

Calculated 1st   Calculation of exponents

Calculated 2nd   Multiplication and division

Calculated 3rd   Addition and subtraction

In the example $4 + .55/4000$, Lotus 1-2-3 performs the math operations in the following order. First 4000 is divided into .55, since division is performed before addition. Next Lotus 1-2-3 adds 4 to the dividend.

You can change the order of calculations by using parentheses. Operations inside parentheses are calculated before any other operations.

QUICK TIP

Some spreadsheet programs use an equal sign (=) for the formula prefix. Lotus 1-2-3 automatically converts an equal sign to a plus sign (+) when the = is used as a prefix.

Using Lotus 1-2-3 functions

Functions are predefined worksheet formulas designed to save you time and enable you to do complex calculations easily. Functions always begin with the formula prefix @ and are called @functions (pronounced "at functions.") Commonly used functions are described in Table 3-5. ▶ Now, use the @SUM function to calculate totals in Pat's worksheet.

1 Click cell **E6**
This is the cell where Pat wants to display the total of all bike tours for June, July, and August.

2 Click the **@function selector button** 📷 as shown in Figure 3-9.
The @function list drops down, displaying a list of functions. To total the values in cells B6, C6, and D6, Pat will use the @SUM function.

3 Click **SUM**
The Contents box and cell E6 display **@SUM(list)**. The information inside the parentheses is called the **argument**. An argument might be a value, range of cells, text or another @ function. To complete this argument, Pat needs to select the range of cells she wants summed, in this case cells B6, C6, and D6.

4 Click cell **B6** and drag to cell **D6**
As you drag to select this range, the pointer shape changes to a 🖉. Notice that the Contents box now displays the range B6..D6 within the parenthesis.

5 Press **[Enter]** to confirm the range and calculate the result
The result of 30 displays in cell E6.

Using the same method you used in steps 1-5 to calculate total bike tours, calculate the three-month totals of raft/canoe, horse, and bus tours. Check your work against the results in Figure 3-10. Then continue to step 6, where you will use the Sum Range SmartIcon to sum the totals for cells E11 and E13.

6 Click cell **B11** and drag to cell **E11**

This selects the range B11..E11. When you use the Sum Range SmartIcon to sum a range, you need to select all the cells you want summed and the empty cell where you want to show the result.

7 Click the **Sum Range SmartIcon** ⊞

The sum of cells B11 to D11 displays in cell E11.

Using the Sum Range SmartIcon, calculate the total for cell E13, which is the total for the 1995 Sales forecast. When you are done, compare your worksheet to Figure 3-10.

FIGURE 3-9: @function selector list

@function selector
button

@function list

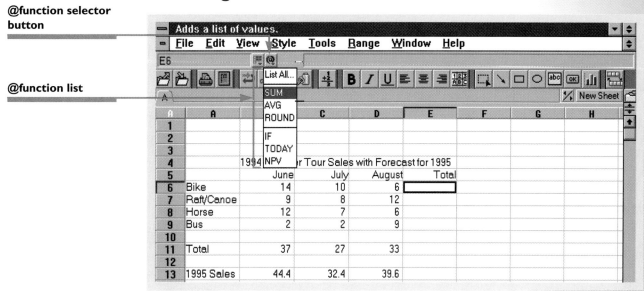

FIGURE 3-10: Worksheet with all functions entered

Contents box shows
function

Sum range SmartIcon

Current cell shows
result

TABLE 3-5:
Commonly used functions

FUNCTION	USE	FUNCTION	USE
@AVG	Calculates the average of a list of values	@SUM	Totals a list of values
@MAX	Displays the largest value in a list of values	@DATE	Formats values as dates
@MIN	Displays the smallest value in a list of values	@TODAY	Displays today's date, according to the computer's system clock

Saving a worksheet

As you build the worksheet, Lotus 1-2-3 keeps the data in the computer's random-access memory, or **RAM**. RAM is temporary storage that is erased each time the computer is turned off or whenever there is a fluctuation in power. To store the worksheet permanently, you must save it to a file on a disk. You should save your work every 10 to 15 minutes and before printing. ▶ Name and save Pat's worksheet to your Student Disk. For more information about your Student Disk, refer to "Read This Before You Begin" at the beginning of this book.

1 Click **File** on the menu bar, then click **Save As**
The Save As dialog box is displayed on the screen, as shown in Figure 3-11.

Next, change the filename from the Lotus 1-2-3 default that displays in the **File name** text box. Edit the text in the File name box the same way you would edit data in a worksheet cell. Lotus 1-2-3 accepts file names consisting of 1-8 characters.

2 Type **TOURS** in the File name text box
The word TOURS displays in the File name text box, replacing the Lotus 1-2-3 default name.

3 Click the Drives list arrow then click the drive that contains your Student Disk
In Figure 3-11, we assume your Student Disk is in drive A. The computer displays an error message if you select a drive that does not contain a disk.

4 Click **OK**
This saves the worksheet as a file named TOURS.WK4. The **default file extension** for Lotus 1-2-3 for Windows worksheets is WK4. The Save As dialog box closes and the filename displays in the title bar at the top of the worksheet.

Next, enter Pat's name at the top of the worksheet.

5 Click cell **A2**, type **Pat Anderson** then press **[Enter]**
The name, displayed in cell A2, indicates who developed the worksheet.

6 Click **File** on the menu bar, then click **Save**
This saves the changes made to a file that already has been named. Save a file frequently while working in it to protect all data. Table 3-6 shows the difference between the Save and the Save As commands.

FIGURE 3-11: Save As dialog box

File name text box

Student Disk Files

Drives list arrow

[Lotus 1-2-3 Release 4 - [Untitled] window with Save As dialog box showing File name "tours", Student Disk Files unit_4-1.wk4, unit_4-2.wk4, unit_4-3.wk4, unit_5-1.wk4, unit_5-2.wk4, unit_5-3.wk4, unit_5-4.wk4, unit_5-5.wk4; File type 1-2-3; Directories a:\; Drives a:; OK and Cancel buttons; Save with password, Selected range only E13..E13]

Selecting the correct drive when saving a file

When you save a file, you need to select the appropriate disk drive on the computer—either drive **a** or drive **b**. Do not save files on the internal hard disk, drive **c** unless you are working on your own computer. Save all your coursework on a disk. To create a back-up copy, save the file on a second disk.

QUICK **TIP**

Click the **Save SmartIcon** for a fast Save, or use the keyboard alternative **[Ctrl][S]** to save your file.■

TABLE 3-6: The difference between the Save and Save As commands

COMMAND	DESCRIPTION	PURPOSE
Save As	Saves file, requires input name	To save a file the first time, change the file's name or save the file for a different application. Useful for back-ups.
Save	Saves named file	To save any changes to the original file. Fast and easy; do this often to protect your work.

Printing a worksheet

Print the worksheet when it is completed to have a paper copy to reference, file, or send to others. Or print a worksheet that is not complete, so that it may be reviewed or worked on when you are not at a computer. Table 3-7 provides printing tips. ▶ Now print a copy of Pat's worksheet.

1 Check the printer
Make sure the printer is on and that it is on-line. If a file is sent to print and the printer is off, an error message results.

Before printing, you can *preview* a file to see what it will look like when printed. For example, if an extensive amount of data is added to the worksheet, it is useful to see if the worksheet still fits on one page. To preview the printed version of a file, use the **Print Preview** option in the next step.

2 Click File on the menu bar, then click Print Preview
The Print Preview dialog box displays.

3 Click OK
A preview image displays, as shown in Figure 3-13. Look at this image to see if the worksheet fits on the page or pages planned. After verifying that the preview image is correct, print the worksheet.

4 Click the Close SmartIcon 🖳
The Close SmartIcon is at the top of the Print Preview window, as shown in Figure 3-13.

When you press the **Close SmartIcon**, Lotus 1-2-3 closes the Print Preview window and displays the worksheet on the screen.

5 Click File on the menu bar, then click Print
The Print dialog box displays as shown in Figure 3-12. Select **Current worksheet** and type **1** at **Number of copies**. Now you are ready to print the worksheet.

6 Click OK
The file is sent to the printer. Note that the **Cancel button** displays on the screen briefly, giving you a chance to cancel the print job.

TABLE 3-7:
Worksheet printing guidelines

BEFORE YOU PRINT	COMMENT
Check the printer	Make sure the printer is on and on-line, that it has paper, and there are no error messages or warning signals.
Check the printer selection	Use the **Printer Setup** command on the **File menu**, to verify the correct printer is selected.
Preview the worksheet	Take a quick look at the formatted image to check page breaks and page setup (vertical or horizontal).

FIGURE 3-12: Print dialog box

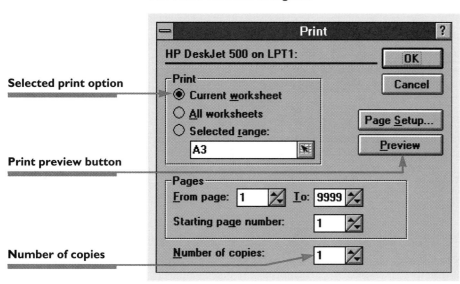

Selected print option

Print preview button

Number of copies

Using Print Preview

The image of the page can be made smaller by clicking on the **Zoom Out**
SmartIcon, or larger by clicking the **Zoom In** SmartIcon, as shown in Figure
3-13. While the image is zoomed in, use the arrow keys to view different sections of
the page.

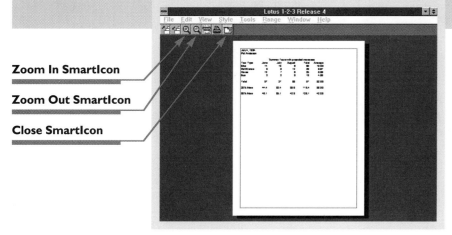

Zoom In SmartIcon

Zoom Out SmartIcon

Close SmartIcon

FIGURE 3-13: Print Preview screen

QUICK **TIP**

Click the **Print
SmartIcon** to open
the Print dialog box.

CONCEPTS REVIEW

Label each of the elements of the Lotus 1-2-3 screen shown in Figure 3-14.

1 _____

2 _____

3 _____

4 _____

5 _____

6 _____

7 _____

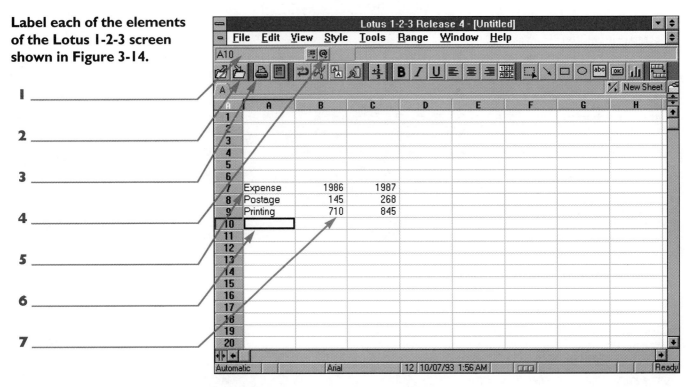

FIGURE 3-14

Match each of the terms with the statement that describes its function.

8 A special predefined formula that provides a shortcut for commonly used calculations

9 A cell entry that performs a calculation in a Lotus 1-2-3 worksheet.

10 A specified group of cells, which may include the entire worksheet.

11 The location of a particular cell in a worksheet, identified by a column letter and row number.

12 The character that identifies an entry as a label and controls the way it is displayed in the cell.

a. Range

b. Function

c. Cell address

d. Label prefix

e. Formula

Select the best answer from the list of choices.

13 The first time you save a new worksheet, which command do you select from the File menu?

a. Save

b. Open

c. Preview

d. Save As

14 You can specify options for printing a Lotus 1-2-3 worksheet by using the:

a. Print manager

b. Print queue

c. Print dialog box

d. Print preview

APPLICATIONSREVIEW

Note: Enter your name and the date on all worksheets.

1 Practice navigating within a worksheet.

  a. Open a new file and, starting from cell A1, press [↓] three times, then press [→] two times to move to cell D5.

  b. Now press [Home] to return to cell A1.

  c. Click cell D7 and watch the cell pointer move to that cell.

2 Enter data in the worksheet.

  a. Click cell A6, type Total then press [Enter].

  b. Click cell B1 and type a caret (^). Notice that the Cancel and Confirm buttons appear in the Contents Box.

  c. Type Share and click the Confirm button to enter Share in cell B1.

  d. Press [→] to move to C1, then type a caret (^) and Price, but do not press the Enter key.

  e. Press [→] to move to cell D1 and note that the centered label Price appears when you move the cell pointer from cell C1.

  f. Type a caret (^) and Sold, then press [Esc] and note that the entry disappears from the cell. Leave cell D1 blank. At this point, your worksheet should look like Figure 3-15.

  g. Compare your worksheet to Figure 3-15.

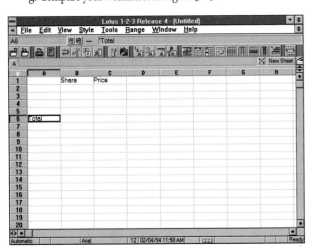

FIGURE 3-15

3 Add data to the existing worksheet.

  a. Enter the four mutual funds labels and values from Table 3-9 into the range A2..C5.

TABLE 3-9

	Shares	Price
Arch	210	10.01
RST	50	18.45
United	100	34.50
Vista	65	11.15

  b. Print the worksheet.

4 Add formulas to the existing worksheet.

  a. Enter a formula to calculate the total number of shares in cell B6.

  b. Save the worksheet as FUNDS and print it.

5 Use functions in the existing worksheet:

  a. In cell C7, use the AVG function to determine the average price of the mutual funds listed.

  b. Type the label Average Price in cell A7.

  c. Save and print this worksheet.

6 Build a simple check register to track debits and calculate the amount spent from an account. Set up the worksheet using the data from Table 3-10.

TABLE 3-10

Check no.	Date	Description	Amount
1601	June 17	Dry cleaning	12.65
1602	June 29	Concert tickets	38.00
1603	July 18	Cable subscription	14.50
1604	July 25	Groceries	47.98

  a. Enter a worksheet title.

  b. Enter the column labels.

  c. Enter all four check numbers, with the corresponding dates, descriptions, and amounts.

  d. Generate a total of the check amounts you have entered. Use the SUM function to display the total in cell D12.

  e. Save the worksheet as CHECKING and close the file.

7 Develop a worksheet that calculates the weekly payroll for Suncoast Security Systems. Set up the worksheet using the data from Table 3-11.

TABLE 3-11

Employee	Hours worked	Hourly wage	Gross pay
D. Hillman	32	9	
S. Lipski	25	12	
L. Skillings	40	7	

a. Enter the column labels, beginning in cell A3.

b. Enter the employee names, hours worked, and wage information.

c. Use a formula to calculate the total number of employee hours worked this week. Enter this total in the appropriate cell.

d. Save the worksheet as SUNCOAST.

8 Enter formulas and use functions in the SUNCOAST worksheet.

a. In the appropriate cells, enter the appropriate formula to calculate the gross pay for each of the three employees.

b. Calculate the total amount of wages that Suncoast will pay out this week. Enter this total in the appropriate column.

c. Using the AVG function, determine the average hourly wage paid to employees at Suncoast.

d. Save and print the worksheet.

e. Close the worksheet.

INDEPENDENT CHALLENGE

You are the box office manager for Lightwell Players, a regional theater company. One of your responsibilities is to track seasonal ticket sales for the company's main stage productions. Lightwell Players sell four types of tickets: reserved seating, general admission, senior citizen tickets, and student tickets.

The 1992-'93 season included productions of *Hamlet*, *The Cherry Orchard*, *Fires in the Mirror*, *The Shadow Box*, and *Heartbreak House*.

Plan and build a worksheet that tracks the sales of each of the four ticket types for all five of the plays. Calculate the total ticket sales for each play, the total sales for each of the four ticket types, and the total sales for all ticket types.

Enter your own sales data, but assume the following: the Lightwell Players sold 800 tickets during the season; reserved seating was the most popular ticket type for all of the shows, except for *The Shadow Box*; no play sold more than 10 student tickets.

To complete this independent challenge:

1 Think about the results you want to see, the information you need to build this worksheet, and what types of calculations must be performed.

2 Sketch a sample worksheet on a piece of paper, indicating how the information should be laid out. What information should go in the columns? In the rows?

3 Build the worksheet by entering a title, the row labels, the column titles, and the formulas. Remember you are creating and entering your own ticket sales data. Do not be concerned about formatting.

4 Save the worksheet as THEATER. Before printing, preview the file so you know what the worksheet will look like. Adjust any items as needed, and print a copy.

5 Submit your worksheet plan, your preliminary sketches, and the final worksheet printout.

UNIT 4

Revising
A WORKSHEET

Building on your ability to create a worksheet and enter data into it, you will now learn how to change the contents of a cell, insert and delete columns and rows, copy and paste information, move cell contents, and resize columns. ▶ In this unit, Pat, from the All Outdoors Tour and Travel Company, decides to modify her worksheet for an upcoming sales meeting. Using Lotus 1-2-3's copy, paste, and move features, she is able to modify the worksheet quickly and effectively. ▶

Opening an existing worksheet

Sometimes it's useful to create a new worksheet by modifying an existing one. This saves you from having to retype duplicate information. To do this, you first open the file you want to modify, and then use the Save As command to save a copy of the file with a new name. Throughout the rest of this book, you will be instructed to open a file from your Student Disk, use the Save As command to create a copy of the file with a new name, and then modify the new file by following the lesson steps. Saving the files with a new name keeps your original Student Disk files intact in case you have to start the lesson over again. ▶ Try opening Pat's Summer Tours worksheet and using the Save As command to create a copy with a new name.

1 Launch Lotus 1-2-3 and make sure your Student Disk is in drive A or B

2 Click **the Open SmartIcon**
   The Open File dialog box displays as shown in Figure 4-1.

3 Click the **Drives drop down list arrow**
   A list of your available drives drops down. Locate the drive that contains your Student Disk. In this lesson, we assume your Student Disk is in drive A.

4 Click **a:** to select the A drive (or click **b:** if your Student Disk is in the B drive)
   A list of files on your Student Disk appear in the filename list box.

5 In the File name list, click **unit_4-1.wk4**
   Compare your screen to Figure 4-1.

6 Click **OK**
   The file named unit_4-1.wk4 opens. To create and save a copy of this file with a new name, use the Save As command. See Table 4-1 for file naming guidelines.

7 Click **File** on the menu bar, then click **Save As**
   The Save As dialog box displays as shown in Figure 4-2.

8 Click the **Drives drop down list arrow**, then click **a:** (or click **b:** if your Student Disk is in drive B)
   A list drops down, displaying your available disk drives. You should save all your files to your Student Disk, unless instructed otherwise. For this lesson, we will assume that your Student Disk is in drive A.

9 In the File Name box, click and drag over the filename **unit_4-1.wk4** to select it (if it is not selected already), then type **smrtours**
   Compare your screen to Figure 4-2.

10 Click **OK**
   The file UNIT_4-1.WK4 closes and is saved on your Student Disk, and a duplicate file named SMRTOURS.WK4 is now open. In subsequent lessons you will be instructed to open a file and save it as a worksheet with a different name. Refer back to this lesson if you need help. Keep SMRTOURS.WK4 open and continue to the next lesson.

FIGURE 4-1: Open File dialog box

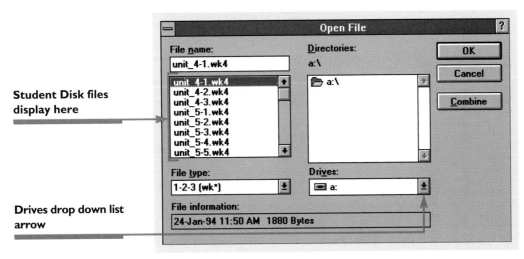

Student Disk files display here

Drives drop down list arrow

FIGURE 4-2: Save As dialog box

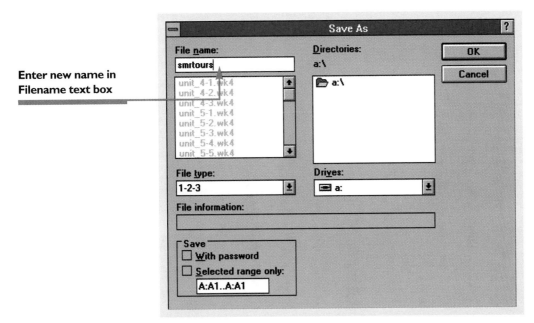

Enter new name in Filename text box

TABLE 4-1: File-naming guidelines

SUBJECT	GUIDELINE
Name	Use up to 8 characters; avoid names that look like cell addresses, function names, or names of keys
Case	Use uppercase, lowercase, or mixed cases
Punctuation	May not be use\d as the first character
Numbers	May not be used as the first character

TROUBLE?

For more information about your Student Disk, read the section at the beginning of this book called "Read This Before You Begin."■

Changing cell entries

Making changes to a worksheet is a two-step process: first you select the cell or range you want to change, then you choose a command to make the desired change. ▶ Pat decides to discontinue bus tours in summer 1995 because of slow sales in 1994. She needs to delete the information relating to buses. She also wants to **format**, or change the appearance of the worksheet title, to make it stand out from the labels.

1 Make sure the worksheet named SMRTOURS is still open
If it is not open, complete the lesson called "Opening an existing worksheet."

2 Select the range **A9..E9**
This selects the bus label and all the bus tour values from June through August.

3 Click **Edit** on the menu bar, then click **Clear**
The Clear dialog box opens as shown in Figure 4-3. Pat wants to clear only the contents and leave the bold formatting in cell A9. This way, if she adds another label to her worksheet, it will display in boldface type. Clicking Style Only would remove any formatting such as bold or italic, but would leave the contents in the cell. Clicking Cell Contents only would remove the contents, but leave any formatting—such as bold or italic—in place.

4 Click the **Cell Contents Only** radio button if it is not already selected, then click OK
Lotus 1-2-3 removes the contents of cells A9 through E9 but leaves the formatting. Anything else you enter in cell A9 would appear in boldface type. Notice that the formula results in rows 11 and 13 change because of the deletion of bus tour sales. Pat now wants to add italic formatting to the worksheet title.

5 Click cell **C4** to select the title 1994 Summer Tour Sales with Forecast for 1995, then click the **Italic SmartIcon** *I*
The title now appears in bold italic. Compare your worksheet to Figure 4-4. Keep this worksheet open and continue to the next lesson.

Clears cell contents, keeps appearance attributes

FIGURE 4-3: Clear dialog box

Clears format, retains content

Clears both contents and format

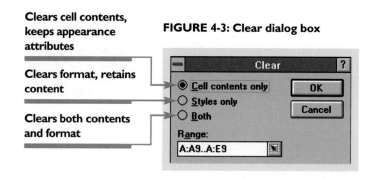

FIGURE 4-4: Worksheet after using Clear command and Italic SmartIcon

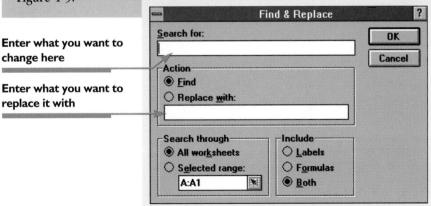

Undo SmartIcon

Italic SmartIcon

Title now appears in
bold italic

Bus tours information
now cleared

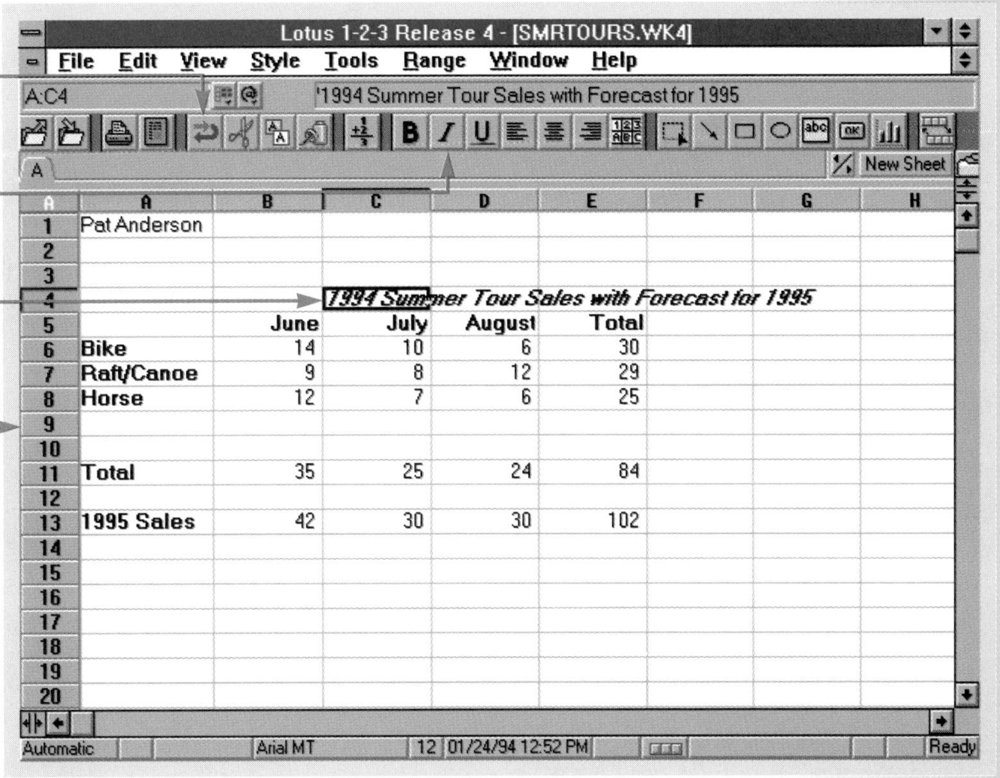

Using Find & Replace to edit a worksheet

Use the Find & Replace command on the Edit menu to make repeated changes to
a worksheet's labels or formulas. Enter the text, values, or formulas you want to
change in the Search for text box. The information that appears here is called the
search criteria. In the Replace with text box, enter the text, values, or formulas
you want to replace the search criteria. The Find & Replace dialog is shown in
Figure 4-5.

Enter what you want to
change here

Enter what you want to
replace it with

FIGURE 4-5: Find & Replace dialog box

TROUBLE?

If you make a mistake
and need to reverse
your last action, click
the Undo SmartIcon
shown in Figure 4-4
or click Undo on the
Edit menu.

Inserting and deleting rows and columns

As you modify a worksheet, you might find it necessary to insert or delete rows and columns. You might have forgotten to include a vital row of information or deleted information and want to close up the gap in data. Deleting or inserting columns or rows can also help to make your worksheet more attractive and readable. ▶ Pat decides to improve the appearance of her worksheet by inserting a row between her worksheet title and the column labels, and deleting the empty row that used to contain bus tour information.

1 Click cell **A5**, then click **Edit** on the menu bar, then click **Insert**
   The Insert dialog box displays, presenting you with the option of inserting a column, row, or sheet. See Figure 4-6. Pat wants to insert a row to add some space between the title and labels.

2 Click the **Row radio button** (if it isn't already selected) then click **OK**
   A blank row is inserted between the title and the month labels. When you insert a new row, the contents of the worksheet shift down from the newly inserted row. When you insert a new column, the contents of the worksheet shift to the right from the point of the new column.

   Now Pat wants to delete the extra row between Horse sales and Total.

3 Move the mouse pointer to the worksheet frame and click the **row 11 selector button** (the gray box containing the number 11)
   This selects all of row 11. If you're not sure where the row 11 selector button is, see Figure 4-7.

4 Click **Edit** in the menu bar, then click **Delete**
   Lotus 1-2-3 deletes row 11, and all rows below this point shift up by one. Compare your worksheet to Figure 4-7. Pat is now satisfied with the appearance of her worksheet and decides to save the changes and close the worksheet.

5 Click the **Save SmartIcon** 📂 to save your changes, then click **File** on the menu bar, then click **Close**

FIGURE 4-6: Insert dialog box

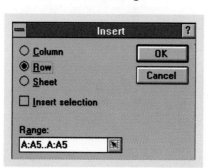

FIGURE 4-7: Worksheet after inserting and deleting a row

Inserted row →

Row II selector button →

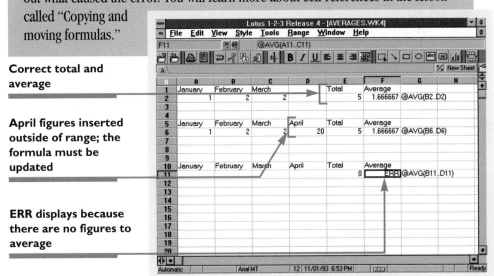

Checking cell references and ranges

If you use cell references or ranges in formulas, you must check your worksheet after you add or delete rows and columns.

When you use a range in a formula and you add or delete columns or rows within that range, Lotus 1-2-3 automatically adjusts the formula to include the new information.

When you add or delete columns or rows outside of a range, you must modify the formula if you want the contents of the added cells to be calculated in the formula, as shown in Figure 4-8. Lotus 1-2-3 displays the special value ERR to indicate that a cell contains an error in the formula. Check the formula's cell references to find out what caused the error. You will learn more about cell references in the lesson called "Copying and moving formulas."

Correct total and average →

April figures inserted outside of range; the formula must be updated →

ERR displays because there are no figures to average →

FIGURE 4-8: Worksheet with ERR

Copying and moving cell entries

Using the Cut, Copy, and Paste SmartIcons or Lotus 1-2-3's drag and drop feature, you can copy or move information from one cell or range in your worksheet to another. ▶ Pat is building a worksheet called Spring and Fall Tours Sales. She has entered all of the labels and values for the Spring report, and is just starting the Fall report. Using the Copy and Paste SmartIcons as well as drag and drop, she will copy information from the Spring report to the Fall report.

1 Open the worksheet from your Student Disk called UNIT_4-2.WK4 and save it as SPGFALL

Pat wants to copy the row labels from the Spring report to the Fall report.

2 Select the range **A6..A11**, then click the **Copy SmartIcon** 🖹

This copies the selected range (A6..A11) and places the copied information on the Clipboard. The **Cut SmartIcon** would remove the selected information and place it on the Clipboard. The **Clipboard** is a temporary storage file which holds all the selected information you copy or cut. To copy the contents of the Clipboard to a new location, you click a new cell, then use the Paste command.

3 Click cell **A15**, then click the **Paste SmartIcon** 🖹

The contents of the selected range are copied from the Clipboard into the range A15..A20, as shown in Figure 4-9. When pasting, you only need to specify the first cell of the range where you want the copied selection to go. Now Pat wants to use drag and drop to copy the Total label from the Spring report to the Fall report.

4 Click cell **E5** to select it, then press and hold down **[Ctrl]**, then slowly move the mouse pointer to the top edge of the cell pointer until it turns into a 🖐

The 🖐 means you can now "grab" the contents of this cell and copy it to another location.

5 While you still hold down **[Ctrl]**, click the left mouse button and drag the cell contents to **E14**

As soon as you click the left mouse button, the pointer shape turns to a ⊕. As you drag, an outline of the cell and the contents moves with the pointer as shown in Figure 4-9. When you release the left mouse button, the Total label displays in cell E14. Pat now decides to move the worksheet title over one cell to the left to make it look more centered.

6 Click cell **C2**, then move the mouse pointer to the top edge of **C2** until it turns to a 🖐, then drag the cell contents to B2

This time the mouse pointer turns into a 🖐 as you drag. This is the pointer shape for moving a cell's contents. See Table 4-2. Pat now needs to enter Fall sales data into the range B15 through D18.

7 Using the information shown in Figure 4-10, enter the sales data for Fall Tours into the range **B15..D18**

Compare your worksheet to Figure 4-10, then continue to the next lesson, keeping your worksheet open.

FIGURE 4-9:
Using drag and drop to copy information from one cell to another

Cut SmartIcon

Copy SmartIcon

Paste SmartIcon

Pointer shape indicates you are copying current cell

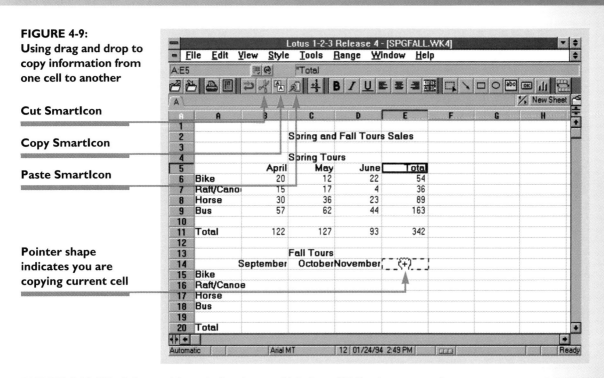

FIGURE 4-10: Worksheet with copied and moved labels and Fall values entered

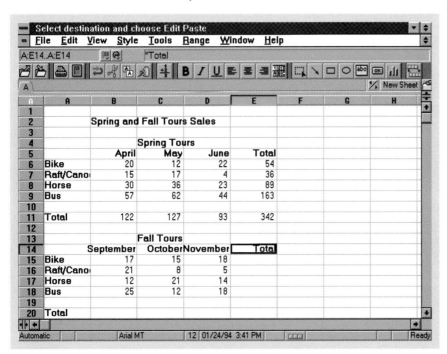

TABLE 4-2: Drag and drop-related mouse pointer shapes

SHAPES	DESCRIPTION
ᗰ	Selects area to copy or move
ᗐ	Indicates that you can now move the selected contents
{+}	Copies the contents of the selected area

QUICK TIP

If you paste into a selected range, the Clipboard contents repeat until the entire range is filled.

Copying and moving formulas

Copying and pasting formulas allows you to reuse formulas you've already created. Copying formulas, rather than retyping them, also helps prevent mistakes. ▶ Pat now wants to copy the formulas from the Spring Tours report to the Fall Tours report.

STEPS ▶

1 Click **E6**, then click the **copy SmartIcon** 🖽
This copies the formula for calculating spring bike tour totals to the Clipboard. Notice that this formula is displayed in the Contents box as @SUM(B6..D6).

2 Click cell **E15**, then click the **Paste SmartIcon** 🖫
The formula from cell E6 is copied into cell E15. A new result of 50 displays in E15. Notice in the Contents box that the cell references have correctly changed, so that the range B15 through D15 appears in the formula. This is because by default, formulas in Lotus 1-2-3 contain relative cell references. A **relative cell reference** tells Lotus 1-2-3 to copy the formula to a new cell, but to substitute new cell references that are in the same relative position to the new formula location. In this case, Lotus 1-2-3 inserted cells D6, C6 and B6, the three cell references immediately to the left of E6.

3 Select the range **E15..E18**
Pat will now use the Copy Down command to copy the formula in cell E15 to cells E16, E17, and E18.

4 Click **Edit** on the menu bar, then click **Copy Down**
See Figure 4-11. The Copy down command copies the formula from the current cell (E15) and pastes it into each cell of the selected range below. Again, because the formula uses relative cell references, E16, E17, and E18 correctly show the totals for Raft/Canoe, Horse and Bus tours. Sometimes you might want a cell reference to always refer to a particular cell address. In such an instance, you would use an absolute cell reference. An **absolute cell reference** always refers to a specific cell address, even if you move the formula to a new location. You identify an absolute reference by placing a $ before the row letter and column number of the address (for example A1). Table 4-3 provides additional information about relative and absolute references. Read through this table, then continue to the next lesson to complete Pat's worksheet.

**TABLE 4-3:
Absolute and relative cell references**

REFERENCE	DESCRIPTION	EXAMPLE
Relative	Used by Lotus 1-2-3 to indicate a relative position in the worksheet. This allows you to transfer formulas from one area to another of the same dimensions. Lotus -1-2-3 automatically changes the column and row number to reflect the new position.	The formula A1 + B1 can be copied to other cells and will use the values of the new location.
Absolute	Contains a dollar sign before the column letter and/or row number to indicate the absolute, or fixed, contents of specific cell(s). This formula may not be applied to other parts of the worksheet although the results of this formula may be incorporated in other formulas.	The formula A1 + B1 calculates only the sum of these specific cells.

FIGURE 4-11: Selected range and Copy Down command

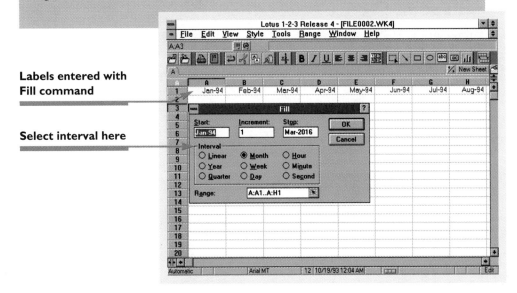

Copy Down command

Formula in E15 will be copied to E16 through E18

Filling ranges

Entering a number of labels can be tedious. With Lotus 1-2-3, you can have the program rapidly enter sequential information in your worksheet by using the Fill or Fill by Example commands on the Range menu. To use the Fill Range feature, first select a range of cells you want to fill, then click Fill on the Range menu. In the dialog box, indicate the interval, start, and stop values. Examples of sequential information include: Monday, Tuesday, Wednesday; January, February, March; or 7, 8, 9. Figure 4-12 shows the Fill dialog box.

Labels entered with Fill command

Select interval here

FIGURE 4-12: Fill dialog box

QUICK **TIP**

Before you copy or move a formula, check to see if you need to use absolute cell referencing.■

Copying and moving formulas, continued

To complete the Fall Tours part of her worksheet, Pat now must copy the formulas from the range B11..E11 to the range B20..E20. To do this, she'll use the Copy and Paste menu commands, and the Copy Right command.

5 Click **B11**, then click **Edit** on the menu bar, then click **Copy**
The edit menu command has the same effect as clicking the **Copy SmartIcon**. See Table 4-4 for cutting, copying, and pasting shortcuts.

6 Click cell **B20**, then click **Edit** on the menu bar, then click **Paste**
The formula for calculating the September fall tour sales displays in the contents box and the result displays in cell B20. Compare your worksheet with Figure 4-13. Now Pat will use the Copy Right command to copy the formula from cell B20 to cells C20, D20, and E20.

7 Select the range **B20..E20**

8 Click **Edit** on the menu bar, then click **Copy Right**
The rest of the totals are filled in correctly. Check your worksheet against Figure 4-14. Pat is done with this worksheet, so she decides to save and close it.

9 Click the **Save SmartIcon** 🖫, then click **File** on the menu bar, then click **Close**

TABLE 4-4: Cut, Copy, Paste, and Undo shortcuts

SHORTCUT	DESCRIPTION
✄	Cuts the contents of the selected area and copies it to the Clipboard
🗐	Copies the contents of the selected area to the Clipboard
🗏	Pastes the contents of the Clipboard
↵	Undoes the last action
[Ctrl] [X]	Cuts the selection and copies it to the Clipboard
[Ctrl] [C]	Copies the selection to the Clipboard
[Ctrl] [V]	Pastes the contents of the Clipboard

FIGURE 4-13: Worksheet with copied formula

Contents box shows
correct cell references

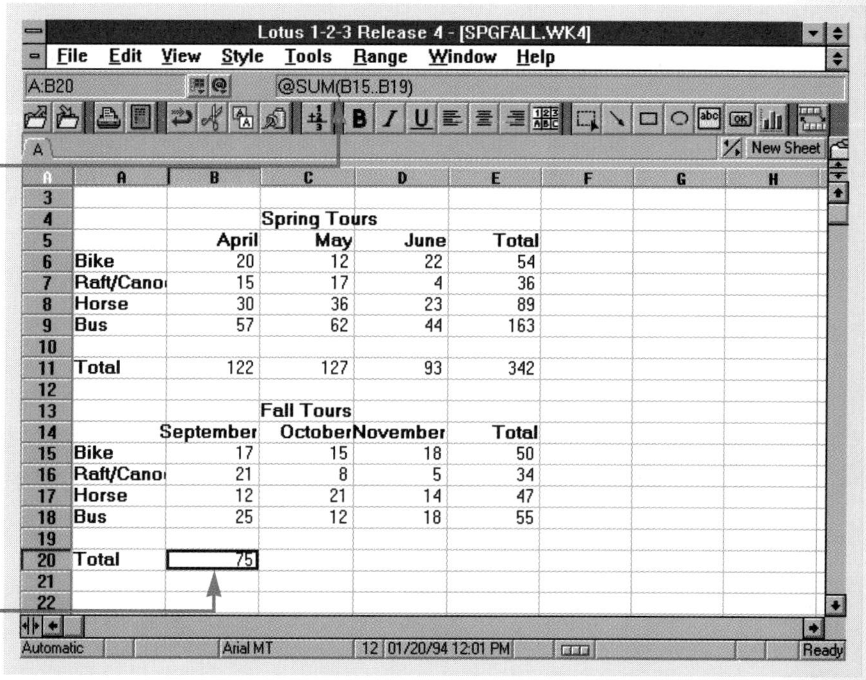

Copied formula
from B11

FIGURE 4-14: Completed worksheet with all formulas copied

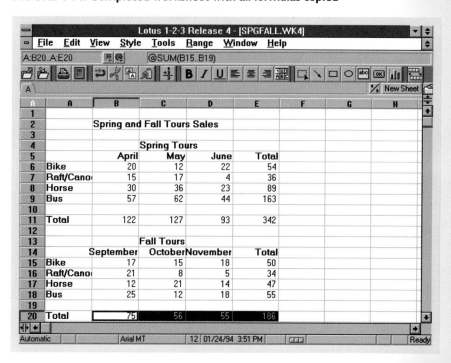

Adjusting column widths

As you enter new information or modify existing information in a worksheet, you may need to adjust column widths to make your worksheet more usable. The default column width is 9 characters wide — less than 1 inch. ▶ With Lotus 1-2-3, you can adjust column width for one or more columns by dragging the mouse or by using the Column Width command on the Style menu. This command allows you to:

- Set the width to a specific number of characters
- Fit the widest entry
- Reset the default widths

Pat looks at several printed worksheets and finds some of the information did not print because the columns are too narrow. She needs to adjust the column widths to make sure the complete labels are printed out.

1 Open the worksheet UNIT_4-3.WK4, then save it as WINTOUR
Refer to the lesson "Opening an existing worksheet" if you have trouble.

2 Click **A2**, then move the mouse pointer to the column line between the A and B column heads
The mouse pointer changes to ✛, as shown in Figure 4-15. You can now make the column wider or narrower.

3 Press the left mouse button and drag the mouse pointer to the right until the contents of Column A are completely displayed
The width of column A is increased and the "Tour Type" labels are easier to read. This might take a few tries because you can't see the results until you release the mouse button.

4 Select **B4..D4**, then click **Style** on the menu bar, then click **Column Width**
The Column Width dialog box displays. Move the dialog box by dragging it by its title bar with your mouse pointer to the bottom of the screen as shown in Figure 4-16 so you can see the contents of the worksheet.

5 Enter 15 in the column width text box then click **OK**
The column widths change to reflect the new settings. You can also use the column width box to make columns fit the widest entry.

Pat is satisfied and decides to save and close her worksheet.

6 Click **File** on the menu bar, then click **Close**, then click **Yes** in the Close dialog box

FIGURE 4-15: Worksheet with default column width

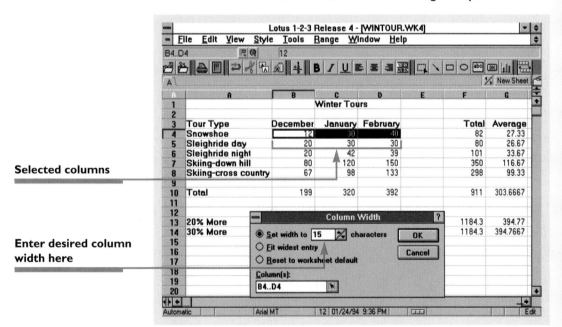

Mouse pointer exactly on the line separating columns A and B

FIGURE 4-16: Worksheet with Column Width dialog box open

Selected columns

Enter desired column width here

Specifying row height

You can also adjust row height to improve readability and allow for larger type-faces. The Row Height command on the Style menu allows you to customize row height. Row height is calculated in **points**, units of measure also used for fonts. One inch equals 72 points. The row height must exceed the size of the font you are using. For example, if you are using a 12-point font, the row height must be more than 12 points.

CONCEPTS REVIEW

Label each of the elements of the Lotus 1-2-3 screen shown in Figure 4-17.

1 _____

2 _____

3 _____

4 _____

5 _____

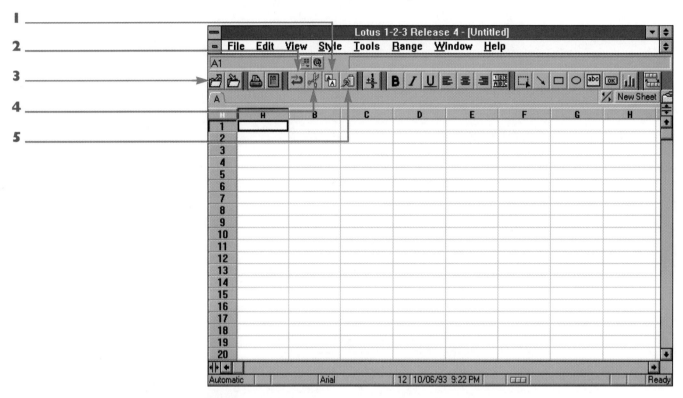

FIGURE 4-17

Match each of the statements to the Edit command it describes.

6 Adds a new row or column in the current worksheet

7 Erases the contents of a cell or range of cells

8 Duplicates the contents of a cell in another cell or range of cells

9 Reverses your most recent action or command

10 Removes a row or column in the current worksheet

a. Undo

b. Delete

c. Insert

d. Clear

e. Copy

Select the best answer from the list of choices.

11 When you copy data using the Copy SmartIcon, Lotus 1-2-3 puts the selected data on the:

a. Border

b. Menu

c. Clipboard

d. Range

12 Which of the following worksheet names will Lotus 1-2-3 accept?

a. 123FILE.WK4

b. MY_FILE.WK4

c. WORKSHEET.WK4

d. !FILE.WK4

13 Cell D4 contains the formula +A4+B4+C4. If you copy this formula to cell D5, what will the formula be in cell D5?

a. +A4+B4+C4

b. +A4+B4+C4-D4

c. +D5-D4

d. +A5+B5+C5

APPLICATIONSREVIEW

Reminder: If you make a mistake, click the Undo SmartIcon ⤺ or use the Undo command on the Edit menu to recover.

1 Create a worksheet in which you will correct cell data.

a. Open a new worksheet and save it as MUSIC.

b. Enter the title B. SHARP INSTRUMENTS, INC. in cell A1.

c. Enter the column headings in cells B3, C3, and D3 using the data from Table 4-5 .

TABLE 4-5
B. SHARP INSTRUMENTS, INC.

	Oct. 1992	Nov. 1992	Dec. 1992
Cellos			
Guitars			
Pianos			
Tubas			

d. Enter the four instruments down the left side of the worksheet in the range A4..A7. The labels Cellos, Guitars, Pianos, and Tubas display in the range.

e. Use the Clear command to remove the contents of cell A7. Only three instruments are now listed on the worksheet.

f. Click cell B4, enter the number 40, then press [Enter]. The value displays in cell B4.

g. Click the Undo SmartIcon to undo your last action. Cell B4 is now empty.

h. Click the Save File SmartIcon to save your work.

2 Use the Find & Replace command to replace dates in the existing worksheet.

a. Click Edit on the menu bar, then click Find & Replace. The Find & Replace dialog box displays.

b. Type 1992 in the Search for box.

c. Click Replace with in the Action list box, then type 1993.

d. Click Selected range in the Search through list box, then type B3..D3.

e. Click OK. Lotus 1-2-3 searches for the criteria you specified and displays a dialog box.

f. Click Replace All. Lotus 1-2-3 replaces all the cells containing the date 1992 with the date 1993.

g. Save your worksheet.

3 Use the Clipboard to copy and paste values in the existing worksheet.

a. Enter the value 50 in cell B4, then press [Enter].

b. Click cell B4, then click Edit on the menu bar, then click Copy. Lotus 1-2-3 copies the selected value to the Clipboard.

c. Select the range B4..C6 then press [Ctrl][V]. Lotus 1-2-3 pastes the Clipboard contents in the selected range of cells. Notice that the keyboard shortcut [Ctrl][V] produces the same result that clicking the Paste SmartIcon would.

d. Enter the value 60 in cell D4, then press [Enter].

e. Use the Copy and Paste SmartIcons to copy the contents of cell D4 to the range D5..D6.

f. Save your worksheet.

4 Use the Copy Down shortcut to copy formulas in the existing worksheet.

a. Enter a formula in cell E4 to calculate the total cello sales during the three-month period. Use cell references, not actual numbers, to build this formula.

b. Position the cell pointer in cell E4, then select the range E4..E6.

c. Click Edit on the menu bar, then click Copy Down. Lotus 1-2-3 copies the formula from cell E4 to the selected range.

d. Click cell E5 and notice the formula in the contents box. Lotus 1-2-3 automatically adjusted the formula so that it calculated the guitar data in row 5.

e. Save your worksheet.

f. Print a copy of the worksheet and close the file.

5 Modify a payroll worksheet.

a. Open the SUNCOAST worksheet that you created in exercise 8 of the Unit 3 Applications Review. If you did not do this exercise, go back and complete it now.

b. Click the cell where L. Skillings is listed in the Employee column.

c. Click Edit on the menu bar, then click Insert. The Insert dialog box displays.

d. Click row, then click OK. A new, blank row displays between S. Lipski and L. Skillings.

e. Enter the new employee, F. Monticello. Notice that the employee list remains in alphabetical order.

f. Enter 40 for Monticello's hours worked, then 11 for his hourly wage.

g. Copy the appropriate formula to calculate Monticello's gross pay.

h. Delete the row containing payroll information for S. Lipski, using the Delete command. Adjust your worksheet formulas as needed.

i. Add the first names of all employees to the Employee column. These are Daniel Hillman, Frank Monticello, and Laurie Skillings.

j. Save your work.

6 Adjust column widths in the SUNCOAST worksheet.

a. Select the range of cells in the Employee column. Lotus 1-2-3 highlights the column that contains a list of Suncoast's employees.

b. Move the mouse pointer into the worksheet area that contains the column letters (A, B, C, and so on).

c. Point at the right border of the column containing the names of Suncoast employees. The mouse pointer changes to a double-ended arrow.

d. Press and hold the left mouse button, then drag the column until the contents of the employee column are completely displayed.

e. Use the Column Width command to fit the widest entry of the Hours Worked column.

f. Try changing the width of some of the columns, by specifying a range that includes cells in the columns you want to change. For example, to change columns B and C, select the range B1..C1.

g. When you are satisfied with the revised worksheet, save your file.

7 Use the drag and drop method to move data in the SUNCOAST worksheet.

a. Select the range of cells containing the entire payroll.

b. Drag the range down by three rows, so that you can add some titles to the worksheet.

c. Enter the company's name in cell A1, then enter the label Weekly Payroll in cell A2.

d. Delete the last action by clicking the Cut SmartIcon, then replace the information by clicking the Undo SmartIcon.

e. Save and print a copy.

f. Close the worksheet.

INDEPENDENT CHALLENGE

As a sales representative for Jason Pharmaceuticals Corporation, you attend many medical conferences all over the country. You have a budgeted expense account for this travel, but at the end of each month, you are required to submit an expense report to your accounting department. This report shows how your actual expenses compare with your budgeted expenses.

Plan and build a worksheet that itemizes your monthly expenses and shows the difference between the budgeted and actual expenses. Include a separate section that shows the total budgeted amount, the total amount spent, and the percentage of budget used.

Your approved monthly travel budget is as follows: $3,000 for airline tickets, $1,500 for lodging, $750 for automobile rental, and $1,100 for meals.

Enter your own data for the actual expenses. You can assume that you did not use all of your allotted budget, except for the car rental, which was $200 over budget.

Then revise the report to reflect a new company-wide policy that allows you to submit up to $100 in miscellaneous travel expenses (parking, dry cleaning, and so on). According to the policy, this expense must appear in the row after the lodging entry on your report.

To complete this independent challenge:

1 Sketch a sample worksheet on a piece of paper, indicating how the information should be organized. How will you calculate the differences between budgeted and actual expenses? What formulas can you copy to save time and keystrokes? Which cell data can you refer to in order to calculate the budget totals and the percentage of budget used?

2 Build the worksheet by entering a title, the row labels, the column titles, and the formulas. Remember to use the budgeted amounts listed above, but enter your own actual amounts.

3 Save the worksheet as EXPENSE. Before printing, preview the file so you know what the worksheet will look like. Adjust any items as needed, and print a copy.

4 Revise the worksheet to insert the new data regarding miscellaneous expenses. Make sure your totals and percentages reflect the new data entry. Save the revised worksheet and print another copy.

5 Submit your preliminary sketches, the original expense report, and the revised expense report.

UNIT 5

OBJECTIVES

▶ Format values

▶ Format cell data with fonts and font sizes

▶ Format cell data with attributes and alignment

▶ Use borders and colors

▶ Use global formats

▶ Check spelling

▶ Freeze rows and columns

Enhancing
A WORKSHEET

You already know how to create a worksheet, how to add or delete information in cells, and how to insert or delete rows and columns. In this unit, you will learn how to use SmartIcons and commands on the Style menu to change fonts, and add colors and borders to create attractive and effective worksheets. You will also learn how to use number formatting to display values as dates, percentages, and currency. ▶ Stefan Swaine, who works in the Marketing Department of the All Outdoors Tour and Travel Company, needs to improve the appearance of several worksheets to make them easier to read and use. ▶

Formatting values

Formatting refers to the way information displays in cells. Formatting does not alter your data in any way. To format a cell, you must first select it, then apply formatting. You can also format a range of cells; this is called **range formatting**. 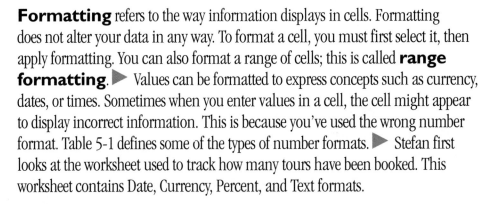 Values can be formatted to express concepts such as currency, dates, or times. Sometimes when you enter values in a cell, the cell might appear to display incorrect information. This is because you've used the wrong number format. Table 5-1 defines some of the types of number formats. ▶ Stefan first looks at the worksheet used to track how many tours have been booked. This worksheet contains Date, Currency, Percent, and Text formats.

1 **Open the worksheet UNIT_5-1.WK4, then save it as BOOKSTUS**
Refer to the lesson in Unit 4 "Opening an existing worksheet" if you have trouble. Stefan needs to enter the booking dates. Before he enters the dates, he will apply the date format to the range **B5..B8**.

2 **Select the range B5..B8, then click Style on the menu bar, then click Number Format**
The Number Format dialog box displays, as shown in Figure 5-1.

3 **Select the format 12/31, then click OK**
You might have to scroll down to see 12/31. Now enter the dates for this range. All these tours were booked on October 24.

4 **Type the date 10/24 in the range B5..B8**
See Figure 5-2. Now apply number formats to the Price information.

5 **Select C5..C8, click Style on the menu bar, then click Number Format, click Currency, then click OK**
Lotus 1-2-3 adds dollar signs and decimal places to the price information. Now you are ready to format column F as percentages.

6 **Select F5..F8, click Style on the menu bar, click Number Format, click Percent, then click OK**
Data in the Percent sold column displays as percentages. Compare your worksheet to Figure 5-2. Stefan is happy with the number formatting and decides to close the worksheet.

7 **Click File on the menu bar, then click Close, then click Yes in the Close dialog box**

TABLE 5-1:
Number formats

NUMBER FORMAT	DESCRIPTION	EXAMPLE
Comma	Inserts comma to separate thousands and decimal for hundreds	123,000.00
Currency	Inserts currency symbol, comma to separate thousands, and decimal for hundreds	$123,000.00
Date	Formats values in a variety of date styles that you can select from the dialog box	Dec 31, 12/31, etc.
Fixed	Indicates plus or minus values with + or −	−123
Percent	Multiplies entry by 100 and inserts percent sign	123%

Scroll to choose a
number format

FIGURE 5-1: Number Format dialog box

Click to reset the
number format

Sample format
displays here

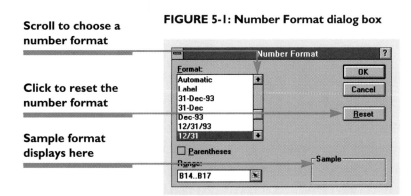

12/31 format

Current format

Percent format

FIGURE 5-2: Worksheet with properly formatted values

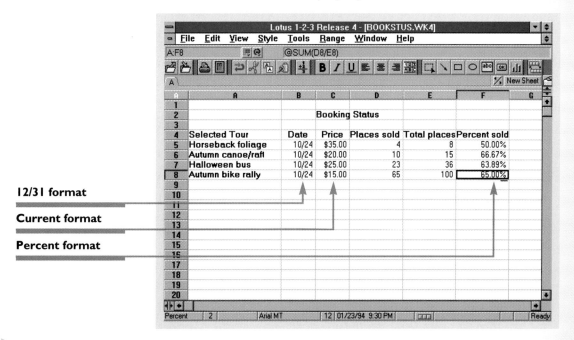

Using the status bar to format numbers

When you select a cell or range of cells, the number format in use displays on the Status bar. You can click this area to display a list of number formats, as shown in Figure 5-3. Make a selection with the mouse then press [Enter].

Click to display list

FIGURE 5-3: Number format list on the status bar

Formatting cell data with fonts and sizes

One of the advantages of working on a computer is that you can change instantly the formatting of text and numbers. **Font** refers to the typeface used to display information in cells. Lotus 1-2-3 uses 12-point Arial MT as the default font to display all cell entries. You can change the font, the size, or both of any entry or section in a worksheet. ▶ Format your worksheet to improve the way it organizes information. For example, the title should be larger than any other text. ▶ Stefan decides to improve the look of the worksheet used for booking tours, by increasing the size of the title and labels. He also explores available fonts.

1   Open the worksheet UNIT_5-2.WK4, then save it as BOOKING

2   Click cell C2 to select the title **Booked Tours**, then click **Style** on the menu bar, then click **Font & Attributes**
Lotus 1-2-3 displays the Font & Attributes dialog box, as shown in Figure 5-4. Scroll up and down through the available fonts and sizes. Stefan decides to keep the default font, Arial MT, but to increase the font size to 24.

3   Click **24** in the Size box, then click **OK**
The title font displays in 24-point type, and the status bar displays the new size information.

Table 5-2 shows several fonts in different sizes. Stefan now decides to make the labels bigger, too.

4   Select **A5..D5**, then click **Style** on the menu bar, then click **Font & Attributes**
Lotus 1-2-3 displays the Font & Attributes dialog box.

5   In the size box, click **14** then click **OK**

6   Using the same process as in Steps 4 and 5, increase the font size to 14 for the ranges **A12..D12, A18..D18,** and **A24..D24**
When you are done, compare your worksheet to Figure 5-5, then continue to the next lesson, keeping your worksheet open.

TABLE 5-2:
Types of formatting

FONT	12 POINT	24 POINT
Helvetica	Lotus 1-2-3	Lotus 1-2-3
Palatino	Lotus 1-2-3	Lotus 1-2-3
Times	Lotus 1-2-3	Lotus 1-2-3

FIGURE 5-4: Font & Attributes dialog box

Current typeface displays here

Available typefaces

Installed sizes

Sample of your selection can be previewed here

Type a custom size or select a size from the list

Click to display under-line options

Click to display a color palette

Click to apply or remove bold, italics, or underline

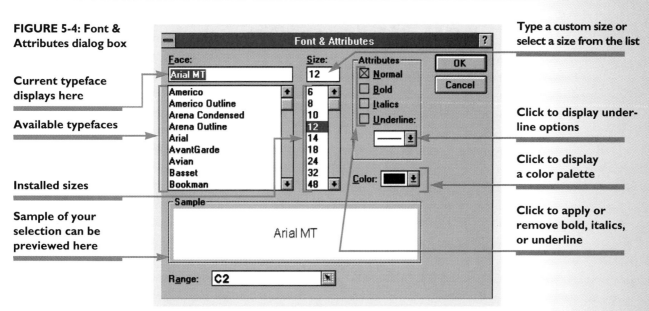

FIGURE 5-5: Worksheet with enlarged title and labels

Title after applying size 24

Status bar displays font and font size

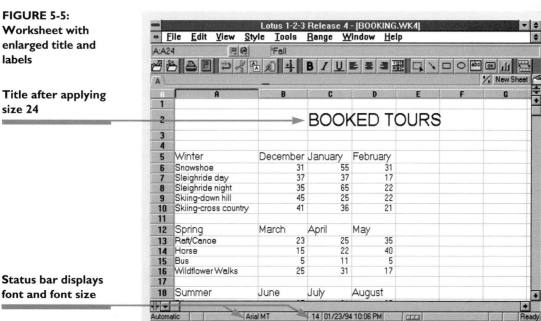

Using the status bar to change fonts and sizes

When you select a cell or range of cells, the font and size displays on the status bar. Click on this description to display a list of fonts or font sizes, as shown in Figure 5-6.

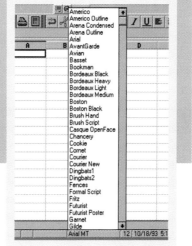

FIGURE 5-6: Font menu on the status bar

QUICK **TIP**

To use a font size that is not listed, type a number in the Size box of the Font & Attributes dialog box and click [OK].■

Formatting cell data with attributes and alignment

Attributes refer to styling features such as bold, italics, and underlining. You can apply bold, italic, or underlining from the Font & Attributes dialog box or by using SmartIcons. Left, right, or center alignment may be applied quickly with SmartIcons, as shown in Table 5-3. ▶ Stefan wants to further refine the worksheet used for booking tours by adding bold and underline formatting and centering some of the labels.

STEPS

1   Make sure the worksheet you saved as BOOKING.WK4 is still open

2   Select the range **A5..D5**, then click the **Underline SmartIcon** U to add underlining

Lotus 1-2-3 underlines the words Winter, December, January, and February. Now on your own, underline ranges A12..D12, A18..D18, and A24..D24. When you are done, continue to Step 4.

3   Click cell **A12**, then click the **Italics SmartIcon** _I_ and **Bold SmartIcon** B

Spring displays in boldface italic type. Stefan decides he doesn't like the italic formatting. He will remove it by clicking the **Italic SmartIcon** again.

4   Click the **Italic SmartIcon**

Lotus 1-2-3 removes italics from Spring. Continue adding bold formatting to the rest of the labels in ranges B12..D12, A5..D5, A18..D18, and A24..D24. When you are done, continue to Step 6.

5   Select **Booked Tours** in cell C2, then click the **Align Center SmartIcon** ≣

The title Booked Tours is centered.

6   Select **A5..D5**, then click the **Align Center SmartIcon** ≣ to center the text in each cell of the range

Now repeat this for each row of labels for the ranges A12..D12, A18..D18, and A24..D24. Compare your results with those shown in Figure 5-7. When you are done, continue to the next lesson.

Careful use of formatting to highlight information on a worksheet can be very useful, but overuse of bold, italics, and underlining can make a document *less* readable. Be consistent, adding emphasis the same way throughout a worksheet or set of documents.

TABLE 5-3:
Common SmartIcons

ICON	DESCRIPTION	ICON	DESCRIPTION
B	Bold	▤	Align left
I	Italic	▤	Align right
U	Underline	≣	Align center

FIGURE 5-7: Worksheet with labels that are bold, underlined, and centered

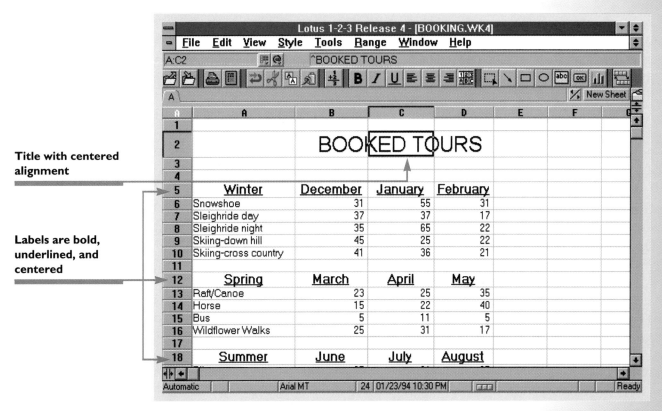

Title with centered alignment

Labels are bold, underlined, and centered

Using named ranges to speed formatting

You can assign a name to a selected range by using the Name command on the Range menu. With a named range, you can select an area to be formatted by typing the name of the range in the Range box of any dialog box. This eliminates the need for typing cell addresses or selecting areas of a worksheet. Once a range is named, you can use that name in formulas, databases, and charts. Figure 5-8 shows the Name dialog box.

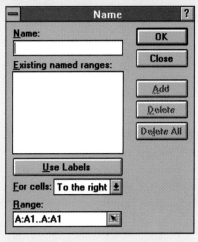

FIGURE 5-8: Name dialog box

QUICK **TIP**

Remove bold, italic, or underlined formats from a selected area by clicking Normal in the Font & Attributes dialog box.■

Using borders and colors

You can also use borders and color to improve a worksheet's readability and usefulness. Color can be applied to the background of columns and rows or to cell contents. Borders are applied by using the **Lines & Color dialog box** on the Style menu. ▶ If your computer does not have a color monitor, the color palette will display in shades of grey. Designer frames located on the bottom of the dialog box provide a palette of alternate borders. ▶ Stefan has decided to add a border and color to the title of the worksheet used for tracking tour bookings.

1   Make sure the worksheet you saved as BOOKING.WK4 is still open

2   Select cells B2..D2 to select **Booked Tours**, then click **Style** on the menu bar, then click **Lines & Color**
Lotus 1-2-3 displays the Lines & Color dialog box, as shown in Figure 5-9. When applying a background color, make sure that you have first selected the entire range in which the label or value displays on the screen.

3   In the Interior box, click the **Background color list arrow**, then choose a color
Lotus 1-2-3 displays a palette of different colors and saturations. When choosing a background color, consider that the more the cell contents contrast with their background, the more readable the contents will be. Stefan chooses yellow for his background color.

4   Click the **Pattern list arrow**, then choose a pattern
Lotus 1-2-3 displays a palette offering different patterns. Choose a pattern that will not obscure the text. Stefan chooses the polka dot pattern.

5   In the Border box, click the **Line style list arrow**, then choose the thickest line
The Sample box previews how your selection will look.

6   Click the **Line color list arrow**, then choose a color for the border
The Sample box previews how your selection will look. Stefan chooses red.

7   At the top of the border box, click **Outline**

8   Click **OK**
The Booked Tours worksheet displays with all your choices for background pattern and color and border color and thickness. Stefan's choices are shown in Figure 5-10. Stefan is now satisfied with his formatting enhancements and decides to save his changes and close the worksheet.

9   Click the **Save SmartIcon** 🖳, then click **File** on the menu bar, then click **Close**

FIGURE 5-9: Lines & Color dialog box

Choose background color, pattern, pattern color, text color, and if negative values should display in red

Background color list arrow

Sample box shows how your choice will look

Select the location, line style, and line color of borders here

Select the type and color of designer frames (custom borders) here

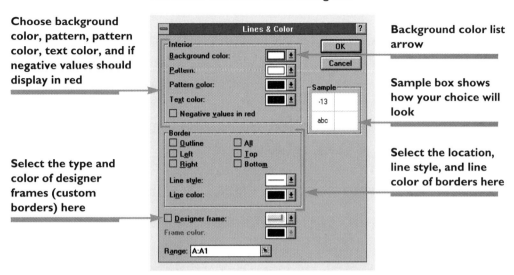

FIGURE 5-10: Worksheet with borders and color formatting

Cells with background color and pattern, and border

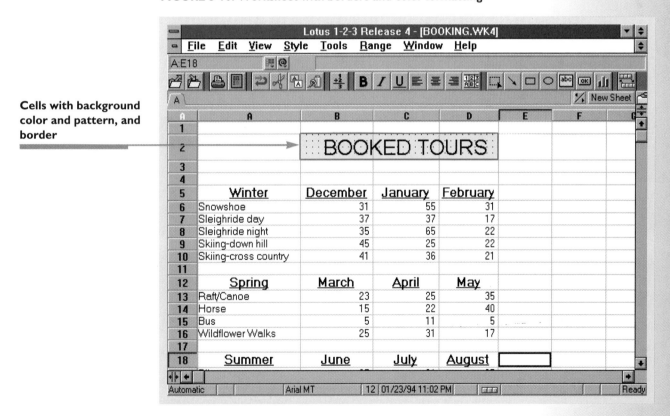

Using color to organize a worksheet

Use color to give a distinctive look to each part of a worksheet, for example, in the BOOKING worksheet. By applying a pale orange to the row for Fall tours, a pale green for Spring, yellow for Summer, and a patterned white for winter, you can set off your material more clearly. To use colors to their best advantage, be consistent throughout a group of worksheets.

TROUBLE?

If a background pattern or color is hiding a cell's contents, change the text color to white.▪

Using global formats

With Lotus 1-2-3, you can apply **global formats**; that is, format an entire worksheet. ▶ Lotus 1-2-3 comes preset with default, or standard, formatting. Default settings make it easier for software users to get to work. These settings include font and size, column width, cell alignment, number formatting, and colors of cell background and text. Worksheet defaults govern the settings of one worksheet. ▶ Stefan looks at a list of employee addresses and decides to change the default settings to make the worksheet more readable. He will change the font setting, and apply text formatting to the phone number column.

STEPS

1 Open the worksheet UNIT_5-3.WK4, then save it as EMPADDR
The worksheet displays with the Lotus 1-2-3 default settings, as shown in Figure 5-11.

2 Click **Style** on the menu bar, then click **Worksheet Defaults**
The Worksheet Defaults dialog box displays, as shown in Figure 5-12. Stefan decides to change the font in this worksheet to Bookman. You might not have this particular font installed on your machine, so choose whatever font appeals to you.

3 Select a font, then type **11** in the Size text box
All text will display in 11-point. Figure 5-13 shows the font changed to Bookman, which was Stefan's choice.

4 Click the **Format drop down list arrow** then click **Text**
This setting will correctly display the Phone Numbers.

5 Click the **Column width up arrow** to **12**
This setting will widen all columns in this worksheet. To decrease column width, click the down arrow.

6 Click **OK**
Lotus 1-2-3 applies all these settings to the entire worksheet, as shown in Figure 5-13. Stefan is happy with the new settings and decides to close the worksheet.

7 Click **File** on the menu bar, then click **Close** then click **Yes** in the Close dialog box
Your worksheet closes, and all settings are saved.

FIGURE 5-11: Worksheet with default settings

Default column widths

Default font 12-point Arial MT

Automatic format treats telephone numbers as calculation

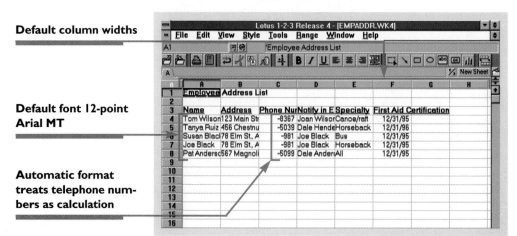

FIGURE 5-12: Worksheet Defaults dialog box

Use this box to set font and size for entire worksheet

Use this box to set column width and alignment

Use this box to set number formats

Use this box to set text color and background color

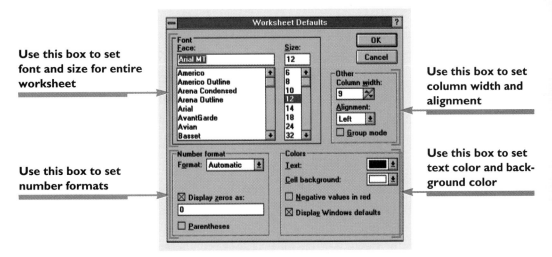

FIGURE 5-13: Worksheet with new default settings

New default column width applied to all columns

New default font, 11-point Bookman

Text format correctly displays telephone numbers

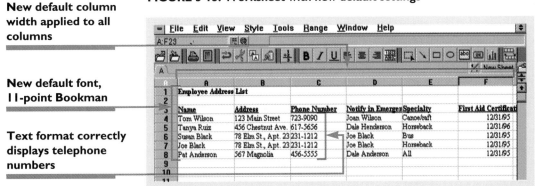

Using collections of ranges to speed formatting tasks

A **collection** is one or more ranges of cells that are selected at the same time. Using collections enables you to apply the same formatting information to ranges of cells, regardless of whether they are next to each other. Figure 5-14 shows two selected ranges that are not adjacent to each other.

To select a collection, select the first range of cells. Press and hold [Ctrl] and select additional ranges.

Collection of ranges

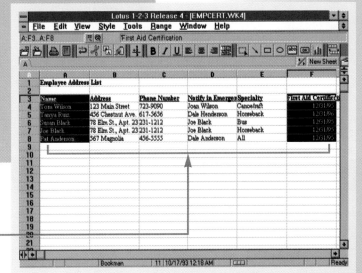

FIGURE 5-14: Selected collection of two ranges

Checking spelling

After you finish formatting a worksheet, you need to check it for spelling errors. ▶ The commercial edition of Lotus 1-2-3 Release 4 for Windows provides a spell check feature, but the Student Version does not. If you are using the Student Version of this software, read this lesson but do not attempt to complete the steps. ▶ You can check for spelling errors in Lotus 1-2-3 worksheets, charts, or selected ranges. It is a good practice to save a worksheet before and after checking spelling. ▶ Proofread all worksheets carefully — the spelling checker looks only for words it doesn't recognize, not for usage errors. For example, the spelling checker would not detect Fine Rats even if you had intended to type Fine Arts. You are responsible for proofreading all values entered in a worksheet. ▶ Stefan now needs to check the spelling of a worksheet showing Winter tours.

1 Open the worksheet UNIT_5-4.WK4, then save it as WINTTOUR

2 Click **Tools** on the menu bar, then click **Spell Check**
   Lotus 1-2-3 displays the Spell Check dialog box, as shown in Figure 5-15.

   Stefan needs to check the spelling of the entire worksheet. Table 5-4 explains other options.

3 Click **Entire file,** then click **OK**
   Lotus 1-2-3 begins checking the entire worksheet for spelling errors. A dialog box displays when Lotus 1-2-3 detects an error, as shown in Figure 5-16.

4 Click **December** in the Alternatives list box, then click **Replace**
   Lotus 1-2-3 replaces the incorrect word and continues checking the worksheet. Continue checking all the spelling. Sometimes Lotus 1-2-3 may not recognize a word and suggest it is misspelled. Choose Skip or Skip All if you do not wish to add it to the dictionary. When Lotus 1-2-3 finishes checking the worksheet, continue to Step 5.

5 Click **File** on the menu bar, then click **Close**, then click **Yes** in the Close dialog box

TABLE 5-4:
Spell Check dialog box
options

OPTION	CHECKS THE SPELLING OF...
Entire file	All cells, charts, and text blocks in the current file
Current worksheet	All cells and text blocks
Range	All cells inside a specified range

FIGURE 5-15: Spell Check dialog box

Choose the area to be checked

Choose different language options here

Click to edit the custom dictionary

Click to display options

Options

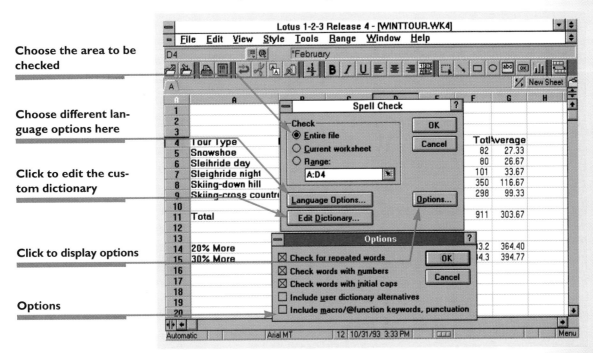

FIGURE 5-16: Spelling error detected

Questioned spelling displays here

Suggested replacement displays here

Alternatives display here

Click to add spelling to dictionary

Click Skip or Skip All if you do not want to change the spelling

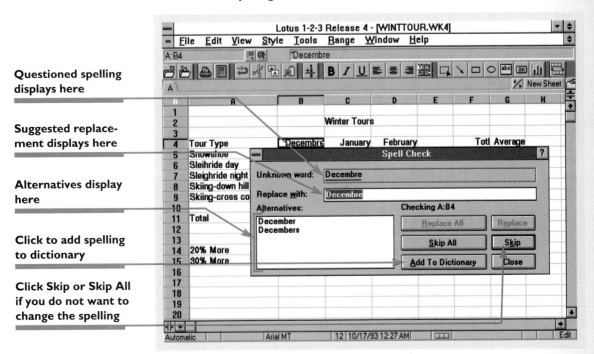

Modifying the dictionary

Your worksheets may repeatedly use words that are not included in the Lotus 1-2-3 dictionary. Add words to the dictionary by clicking the Add To Dictionary button when Lotus 1-2-3 suggests a word is incorrect.

Freezing rows and columns

As a worksheet fills up with information, you will need to scroll through the file more often just to view information. Looking at information without labels can be frustrating. With Lotus 1-2-3, you can freeze columns and rows in place and scroll through the rest of your worksheet while still viewing the labels. Freezing rows and columns is especially useful when you're working with large worksheets. ▶ Due to a high-volume of bike tours sold for April, Dale Henderson in Operations has been asked to check March inventory levels for bike-related gear.

1 **Open the worksheet Unit_5-5 and save it as INVENT'Y.WK4**
Dale needs to view the March inventory levels, which are not currently visible in the worksheet window. She will have to freeze column A to be able to read the inventory items and view the information in the March column. To freeze a column, click anywhere in the column to the right of the one you want to freeze.

2 **Click cell B7, then click View on the menu bar, then click Freeze Titles**
The Freeze titles dialog box displays, as shown in Figure 5-17.

3 **Click columns, then click OK**
Dale can now scroll to the right and still be able to view the inventory items listed in column A.

4 **Click the right scroll arrow on the horizontal scroll bar until March displays on your screen**
Now Dale can view the March column and all the labels for the inventory items in column A. She notes that the levels for bike kits, bikes, and air pumps are all rather low, so she makes a note to reorder those items. She now needs to check the inventory levels for water bottles. To view the labels and the inventory volumes for this item, she will have to freeze both column A and the row containing the months labels. To do this, she first must unfreeze the column A titles, and scroll back to column A.

5 **Click View on the menu bar, then click Clear Titles, then scroll back to the left until column A is in view**
Column A is no longer frozen.

6 **Click cell B7, then click View on the menu bar, then click Freeze Titles, then click Both then click OK**
Now Dale can scroll anywhere in the worksheet and still view the labels for months and inventory items.

7 **Click the down arrow on the vertical scroll bar until water bottles comes into view, then press [Tab]**
Pressing Tab moves you one screen to the right. You should now be able to view the label for March, the label for water bottles, and the value for the inventory level in cell K27, which is 8. Check your screen against Figure 5-18. Dale makes a note to reorder this item. Satisfied with this information, she can unfreeze the titles and close the worksheet.

8 **Click View on the menu bar, then click Clear Titles**
The titles unfreeze.

9 **Click File on the menu bar, then click Close, then click Yes to save your worksheet**

FIGURE 5-17: Freeze Titles dialog box

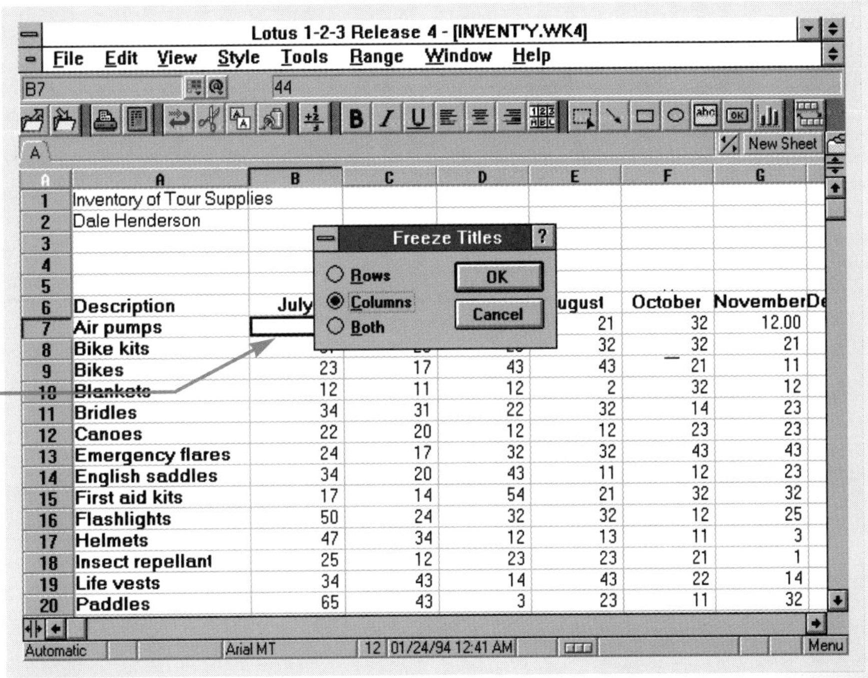

Click a cell in Column
B to freeze column A

FIGURE 5-18: Scrolled worksheet with frozen row and column

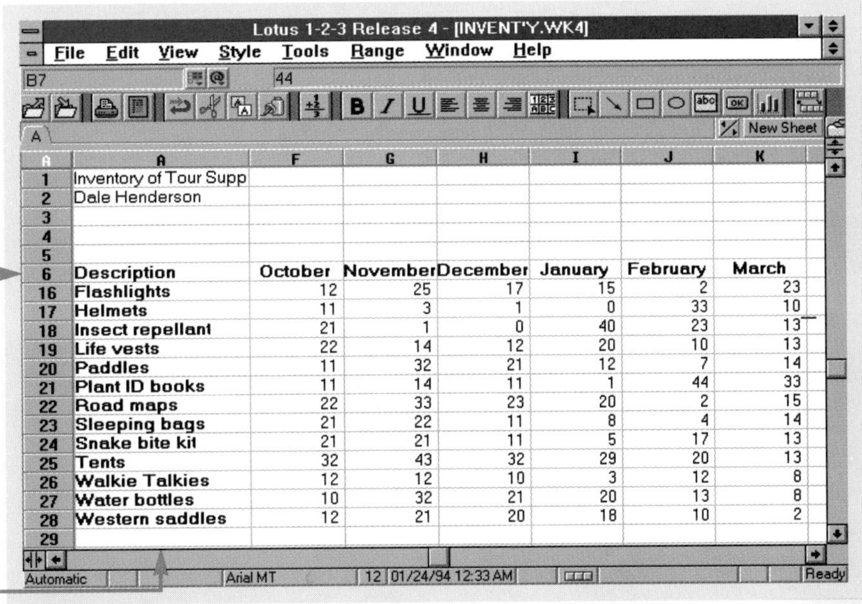

Row 6 is frozen

Column A is frozen

Editing frozen titles

Once titles are frozen, you do not want to unfreeze and then refreeze them in order to make edits or corrections. Press [F5] and enter a cell address to move to a cell or range in the frozen area. The column or row of titles is duplicated. Edit the set where the cell pointer displays.

After correcting a row, press [Ctrl] [←] and then [Ctrl] [→].

After correcting a column, press [PgDn] and then [PgUp].

QUICK **TIP**

Use [Tab] and [Shift] [Tab] to scroll horizontally one screen at a time.■

CONCEPTSREVIEW

Label each of the elements of the Lotus 1-2-3 screen shown in Figure 5-19.

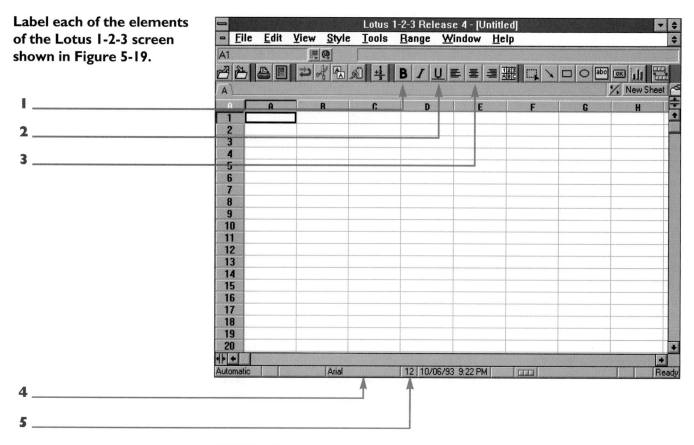

1 _____

2 _____

3 _____

4 _____

5 _____

FIGURE 5-19

Match each of the statements with the Style menu command it describes.

6 Modifies the horizontal positioning of cell data

7 Adds borders to worksheet cells

8 Sets default styles for the current worksheet

9 Changes the typeface and point size of text

10 Changes the display format of values in cells

a. Font & Attributes

b. Alignment

c. Number Format

d. Lines & Color

e. Worksheet Defaults

Select the best answer from the list of choices.

11 The number 5707 formatted with Currency and two decimal places displays as:

a. $5707

b. $5707.00

c. $57.07

d. $5,700.00

12 When you apply the Worksheet Defaults command, it affects:

a. A single cell

b. A single row

c. A single column

d. The entire worksheet

APPLICATIONSREVIEW

1 Build an inventory report.

a. Open a new worksheet.

b. Enter the information from Table 5-5 in your worksheet.

TABLE 5-5

Country Oak Chairs, Inc.
Quarterly Sales Sheet

Description	Price	Sold
Rocker	1299	1104
Recliner	800	1805
Bar stool	159	1098
Dinette	369	1254

c. Save the worksheet as CHAIRS to your Student Disk.

2 Format dollar amounts in the existing worksheet.

a. Select the range of cells in the Price column.

b. Click Style in the menu bar then click Number Format. The Number Format dialog box displays.

c. Click Currency in the list box.

d. Click 2 in the Decimal Places text box.

e. Click OK. The numbers in the Price column are displayed with a currency symbol ($) and two decimal places.

f. Save your worksheet.

3 Use the Comma format in the existing worksheet.

a. Select the range of cells in the Sold column.

b. Format the range using the Comma format with no decimal places. The numbers in the Sold column display with commas.

c. Enter a formula in the appropriate cell to calculate the total number of chairs sold. Adjust the number formatting, as needed.

d. Enter the label Total in the cell next to it.

e. Save your worksheet.

4 Format labels in the existing worksheet.

a. Select the worksheet title, Country Oak Chairs, Inc.

b. Click the Bold SmartIcon to apply boldface to the worksheet title.

c. Select the label Quarterly Sales Sheet.

d. Click the Underline SmartIcon to apply underlining to the label.

e. Select the range of cells containing the column titles.

f. Click the Align Center SmartIcon to center the column titles.

g. Save your work.

5 Use borders and color in the existing worksheet.

a. Select the cell containing the total number of chairs sold.

b. Click Style in the menu bar, then click Lines & Color.

c. Check All in the Border list box, then select an appropriate line style and line color.

d. Click OK. The data is displayed with the selected border.

e. Select the worksheet title, Country Oak Chairs, Inc., then click Style on the menu bar, then click Font & Attributes.

f. Use the Color palette to select a font color.

g. Practice applying color to the worksheet column titles and the row labels.

h. Save and close the worksheet.

6 Format a report.

a. Open a new worksheet and use the Save As command to name it NPR.

b. Enter the information from Table 5-6 in your worksheet.

TABLE 5-6

National Public Radio contributions

City	Pledged	% Received
Honolulu	63000	.75
New York	42000	.63
San Francisco	45750	.54
Boston	52950	.52
Seattle	60000	.81

c. Change all of the column widths to 12 characters.

d. Use the Currency format with two decimal places for the numbers in the Pledged column.

e. Use the Percent format with no decimal places for the numbers in the % Received column.

f. Change the width of the City column to 14 characters.

g. Make the worksheet title bold.

h. Save your worksheet.

7 Change fonts and check spelling in the existing worksheet

   a. Select the worksheet title.

   b. Click Style in the menu bar, then click Font & Attributes.

   c. Select Times from the Face list box, then select 18 from the Size list box.

   d. Look in the sample box to see how the selection will display, then click OK.

   e. Now change all of the column titles to 14 point Times.

   f. Click Tools in the menu bar, then click Spell Check.

   g. Check the spelling for the entire worksheet file, then save your worksheet.

8 Freeze a row in the existing worksheet.

   a. Enter the names of cities down the left side of the worksheet, directly under the Seattle entry. Continue entering names until you can no longer view the entire screen without scrolling.

   b. Place your cell pointer just below the row containing the column titles (City, Pledged, % Received).

   c. Click View in the menu bar, then click Freeze Titles, click Rows, then press [Enter].

   d. Scroll down the worksheet and notice that the labels stay on the top of the screen.

   e. Save and close the worksheet.

INDEPENDENT
CHALLENGE

W rite Brothers is a Houston-based company that manufactures high-quality pens and markers. As the finance manager, one of your responsibilities is to analyze the monthly reports from your five district sales offices. Your boss, Joanne Parker, has just told you to prepare a quarterly sales report for an upcoming meeting. Since several top executives will be attending this meeting, Joanne reminds you that the report must look professional. In particular, she asks you to emphasize the company's surge in profits during the last month and to highlight the fact that the Northeastern district continues to outpace the other districts.

Plan and build a worksheet that shows the company's sales during the last three months. Make sure you include:

- The number of pens sold (units sold) and the associated revenues (total sales) for each of the five district sales offices. The five Write Brothers sales districts include: Northeastern, Midwestern, Southeastern, Southern, and Western.

- Calculations that show month-by-month totals and a three-month cumulative total

- Calculations that show each district's share of sales (percent of units sold)

- Formatting enhancements to emphasize the recent month's sales surge and the Northeast district's sales leadership.

To complete this independent challenge:

1 Prepare a worksheet plan that states your goal, lists the worksheet data you'll need, and identifies the formulas for the different calculations.

2 Sketch a sample worksheet on a piece of paper, indicating how the information should be formatted. How will you make the numbers easy to read? How will you show dollar amounts? What information should be shown in bold? What information will require a border around it? Do you need to use more than one font? More than one point size?

3 Build the worksheet with your own sales data. Enter the titles and labels first, then enter the numbers and formulas. Save the worksheet as PENS.

4 Make enhancements to the worksheet. Format labels and values, change attributes and alignment, and add borders. Remember to check your spelling.

5 Before printing, preview the file so you know what the worksheet will look like. Adjust any items as needed, and print a copy. Save your work before closing the file.

6 Submit your worksheet plan, preliminary sketches and the final worksheet printout.

UNIT 6

OBJECTIVES

▶ Plan and design a chart

▶ Create a chart

▶ Change chart types

▶ Move and resize a chart

▶ Enhance a chart

▶ Save and print a chart

Working
WITH CHARTS

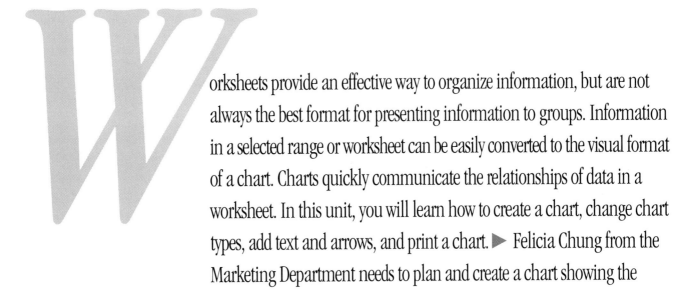

orksheets provide an effective way to organize information, but are not always the best format for presenting information to groups. Information in a selected range or worksheet can be easily converted to the visual format of a chart. Charts quickly communicate the relationships of data in a worksheet. In this unit, you will learn how to create a chart, change chart types, add text and arrows, and print a chart. ▶ Felicia Chung from the Marketing Department needs to plan and create a chart showing the 6-month sales history of a new tour program. ▶

Planning and designing a chart

Before creating a chart, you need to plan what you want your chart to show, and how you want it to look. ▶ Felicia Chung from Marketing wants to create a chart showing spring and summer sales of a new tour series called Thrill Seeker tours. These three tours include a parachute dive from a small-engine aircraft, a bungee jump off a cliff, and a flight on a hang glider into a canyon. In early June, Felicia launched a TV advertising campaign promoting the three different Thrill Seeker tours which resulted in increased sales for the summer months. Felicia wants her chart to illustrate this dramatic sales increase. Using Figure 6-1 and the guidelines below, follow Felicia as she plans her chart.

■ Determine the purpose of the chart, and identify the data relationships you want to communicate visually.

Felicia wants to create a chart that shows sales of Thrill Seeker tours in the spring and summer months (March through August). She particularly wants to highlight the increase in sales that occurred in June as a result of her advertising campaign.

■ Determine the results you want to see and decide which chart type is most appropriate to use. Table 6-1 describes several different types of charts.

Because Felicia wants to compare related data (sales of Thrill Seeker tours) over a time period (the months March through August), she decides to use a bar chart.

■ Identify the worksheet data you want the chart to illustrate.

Felicia will use data from her worksheet titled "Thrill Seeker Tours, Spring and Summer Sales," shown in Figure 6-1. This worksheet contains all the sales data for parachute, bungee jump, and hang glide tours from March through August.

■ Make a rough sketch that shows how the chart will look. Use this sketch to decide where the chart elements should be placed.

*Felicia sketches her chart as shown in Figure 6-1. She puts the months on the horizontal axis (called the **x-axis**) and the number of tours sold on the vertical axis (called the **y-axis**). She puts **tick marks** on the y-axis to create a scale of measure for each value. Each value in any cell she selects for her chart is called a **data point**, and a collection of related data points is called a **data series**. In Felicia's chart, there are three data series (bungee jump, parachute, and hang glide) so she has included a **legend** to identify them. In any chart, each data point is visually represented by a **data marker**, which in this case is a bar.*

TABLE 6-1:
Types of charts

	TYPE	DESCRIPTION
	Bar	Compares the relationship between specific amounts of data over one time period or over a few time periods, such as four quarters. Bar charts can be horizontal or vertical.
	Line	Shows changes in data or categories of data over longer periods of time. A line chart is effective when you want to document trends. Newspapers, for example, use them to chart stock market trends.
	Area	Is similar to a line chart, but uses the areas between lines to emphasize the relationship of data to each other.
	Pie	Shows the relationship of parts to a whole. A pie chart is useful when you want to express data as percentages.

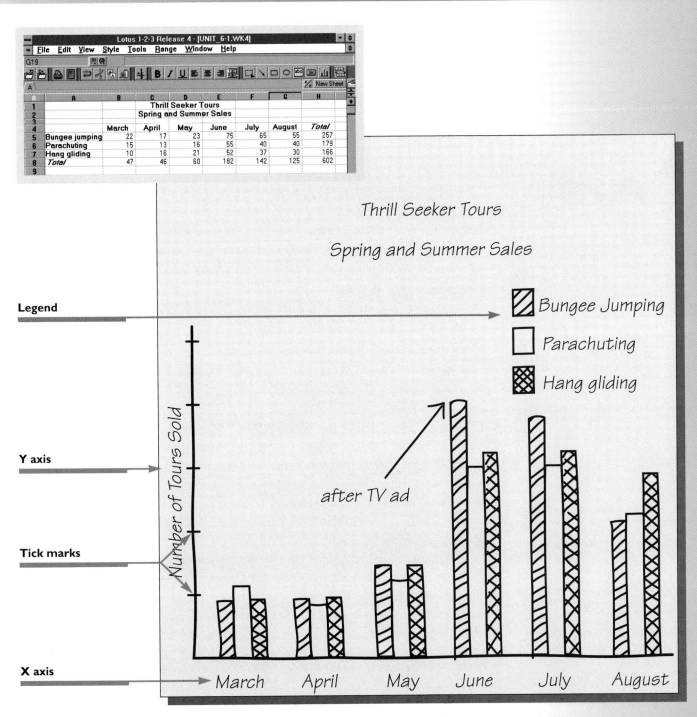

FIGURE 6-1: Worksheet and hand-drawn sketch of chart

Creating a chart

To create a chart, you first need to select the cells in your worksheet that you want to chart. Once you've selected a range, you can click the Chart SmartIcon to create a chart automatically ▶ Felicia opens the worksheet containing spring and summer sales data for the Thrill Seeker tour series. She will now create a chart that shows the monthly sales of each type of Thrill Seeker tour from March through August.

1   Open the worksheet **UNIT_6-1.WK4** from your Student Disk, then save it as **THRILLS.WK4**

Felicia needs to select the cells she wants to chart. She wants to include the monthly sales figures for each of the tour types, but she does not want to show any of the totals. She also wants to include the worksheet title and the month and tour type labels.

2   Select the range **A1..G7**

This range contains the worksheet title, the tour type and month labels, and the values that express monthly sales figures for each tour type.

3   Click the **Chart SmartIcon** 📊

Clicking the Chart SmartIcon makes the mouse pointer change to a 📊 as shown in Figure 6-2. Felicia needs to click the location where she wants the chart to appear. Felicia decides to place the chart directly below the worksheet.

4   Click the upper left corner of cell **A9**

A bar chart displays just below the worksheet, with cell A9 containing the upper left corner of the chart. Felicia is pleased with the chart. Just as she wanted, it shows the dramatic increase in sales between May and June. She also notices that the chart has incorporated many elements from the selected worksheet cells, including a **title** ("Thrill Seeker Tours"), a subtitle ("Spring and Summer Sales"), the month **labels** just above the x-axis, and a **legend** showing each tour type data series and its corresponding color on the chart. The chart is now selected, which you can tell by the presence of selection handles. **Selection handles** are the small black squares at the corners and sides of the chart's outer edge that allow you to move and resize the chart easily. To select a chart, click in a blank space inside the chart frame. To deselect a chart, click anywhere outside the chart. Anytime the chart is selected (as it is now), the chart SmartIcon palette displays chart-related SmartIcons. Keep this worksheet open and continue to the next lesson.

TABLE 6-2: Charting terms

TERM	DEFINITION
Chart title	Name of a chart
Data series	The graphic rendition of a selected range in a worksheet
Legend	A box explaining the colors or patterns
X-axis	The horizontal line in a chart or graph
X-axis label	Label describing the x-axis
Y-axis	The vertical line in a chart or graph
Y-axis label	Label describing the y-axis

FIGURE 6-2:
Worksheet with selected cells and chart pointer

Selected range

Chart pointer

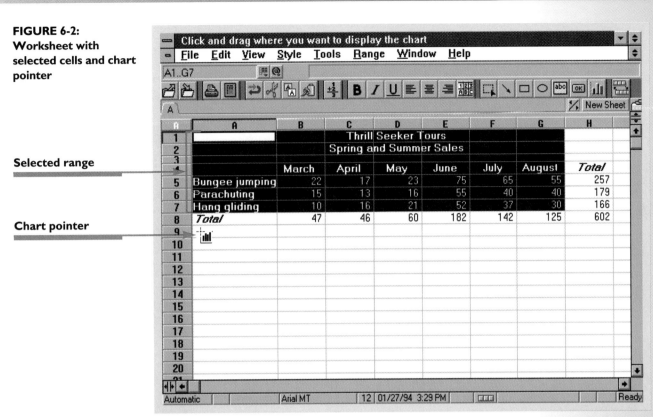

FIGURE 6-3:
Worksheet with bar chart

Selection handles

Title and subtitle

Month labels on x-axis

Legend

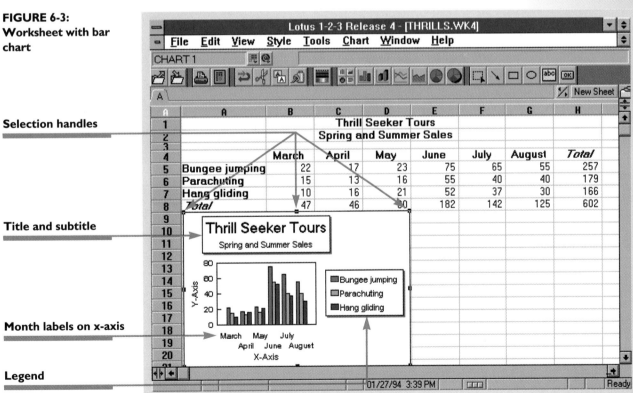

QUICK **TIP**

To delete a chart, select it and press **[Del]**.■

Changing chart types

Whenever you create a new chart, Lotus 1-2-3 inserts a bar chart by default. Using the Chart SmartIcons, however, it's easy to change chart types. Table 6-3 shows and describes all the Chart SmartIcons. Familiarize yourself with these SmartIcons before continuing. ▶ Felicia wants to find out what percentage of total sales the month of June represents. She will convert the bar chart to a pie chart to find this out.

1 Make sure the **THRILLS.WK4** worksheet is still open

2 Select the chart (if it is not already selected) by clicking any blank space inside the chart frame

3 Click the **Chart Type SmartIcon** 🖳
The Type dialog box displays, as shown in Figure 6-4. Clicking any of the chart type radio buttons in the Types box displays a small picture of what your chart would look like in that format. Felicia wants to find out the percentages that each month contributed to the whole selling period, so she is going to choose a pie chart format.

4 Click **Pie** in the Types box, then Click **OK**
The bar chart changes to a pie chart, as shown in Figure 6-5. Felicia can now immediately see the percentage that each month contributed to the total sales. The yellow wedge representing June sales shows more than a quarter of the total pie (29.2%). The green wedge, representing April sales, shows just a tiny sliver. Felicia looks at the pie chart and takes some notes, and then decides to convert it back to a bar chart, for the sales meeting. This time, however, she decides she wants to use a three-dimensional bar chart format.

5 Click the **3-D Bar Chart SmartIcon** 🖳
A three-dimensional bar chart displays as shown in Figure 6-6. Keep this worksheet open and continue to the next lesson.

TABLE 6-3:
Chart SmartIcons

ICON	DESCRIPTION
🖳	Opens Lines & Color dialog box
🖳	Opens Type dialog box from Chart menu
🖳	Displays selected chart as bars
🖳	Displays selected chart as 3D bars
🖳	Displays selected chart as line chart
🖳	Displays selected chart as area chart
🖳	Displays selected chart as pie chart
🖳	Displays selected chart as 3D pie chart

FIGURE 6-4:
Type dialog box

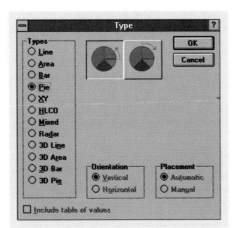

FIGURE 6-5:
Worksheet with pie chart

Chart Type SmartIcon

3-D bar chart SmartIcon

Pie chart

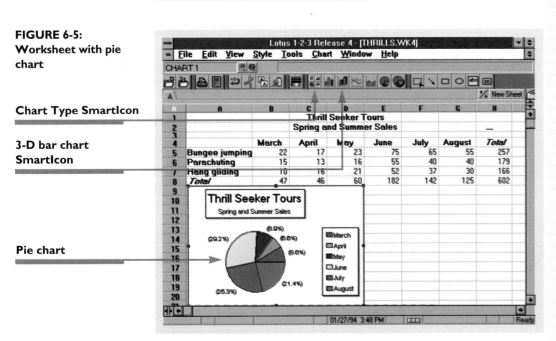

FIGURE 6-6:
Worksheet with three-dimensional bar chart

3-D Bar Chart SmartIcon

Three-dimensional bar chart

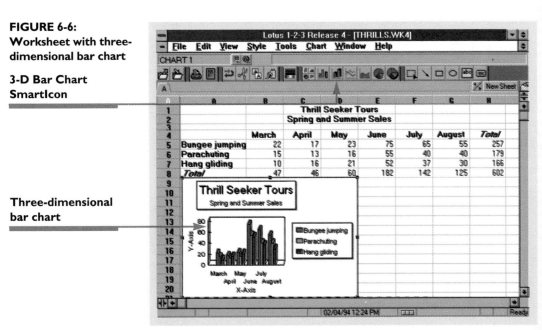

Moving and resizing a chart

Charts are graphics, or drawn **objects**, and have no specific cell or range address. You can move charts anywhere on a worksheet without affecting formulas or data in the worksheet. You can also easily resize a chart to improve its appearance by dragging the selection handles. Charts contain many elements, each of which are separate objects that you can move and resize. To move or resize an object, first select it, then drag it to a new location or use the selection handles to resize it. ▶ Felicia wants to increase the size of her bar chart and then move it to a more centered location on her worksheet. She also wants to move the legend up so that it is level with the title.

1 Make sure the worksheet THRILLS.WK4 is still open and the chart is selected

2 Move the mouse pointer over the selection handle on the outer right edge of the chart until the pointer changes to a ✥
The ✥ pointer shape indicates that you can now click and drag the chart to resize it.

3 Hold down the left mouse button and drag the right border of the chart to the right edge of the F column, then release the mouse button
The chart width is increased. Notice that all the month labels now are aligned on the same level, and the chart is much easier to read. Now Felicia wants to move the chart so that it is more centered under the worksheet.

4 Select the chart (make sure the selection handles appear on the outer edge of the chart), then hold down the left mouse button, then drag the chart about a half inch over to the right
The pointer shape changes to a ⌐⌐⌐ as shown in Table 6-4. The chart should now be centered in the worksheet. Felicia now decides to move the legend box up so that it is level with the chart title.

5 Click the legend to select it, then drag it to the upper right corner of the chart, as shown in Figure 6-7
Several selection handles appear when you click the legend, and the mouse pointer changes to a ⌐⌐⌐ when you drag. Keep your worksheet open and continue to the next lesson.

TABLE 6-4: Mouse-pointer shapes

SHAPE	DESCRIPTION
✥	Allows you to resize a chart
⌐⌐⌐	Allows you to drag and drop

FIGURE 6-7: Worksheet with repositioned chart and legend

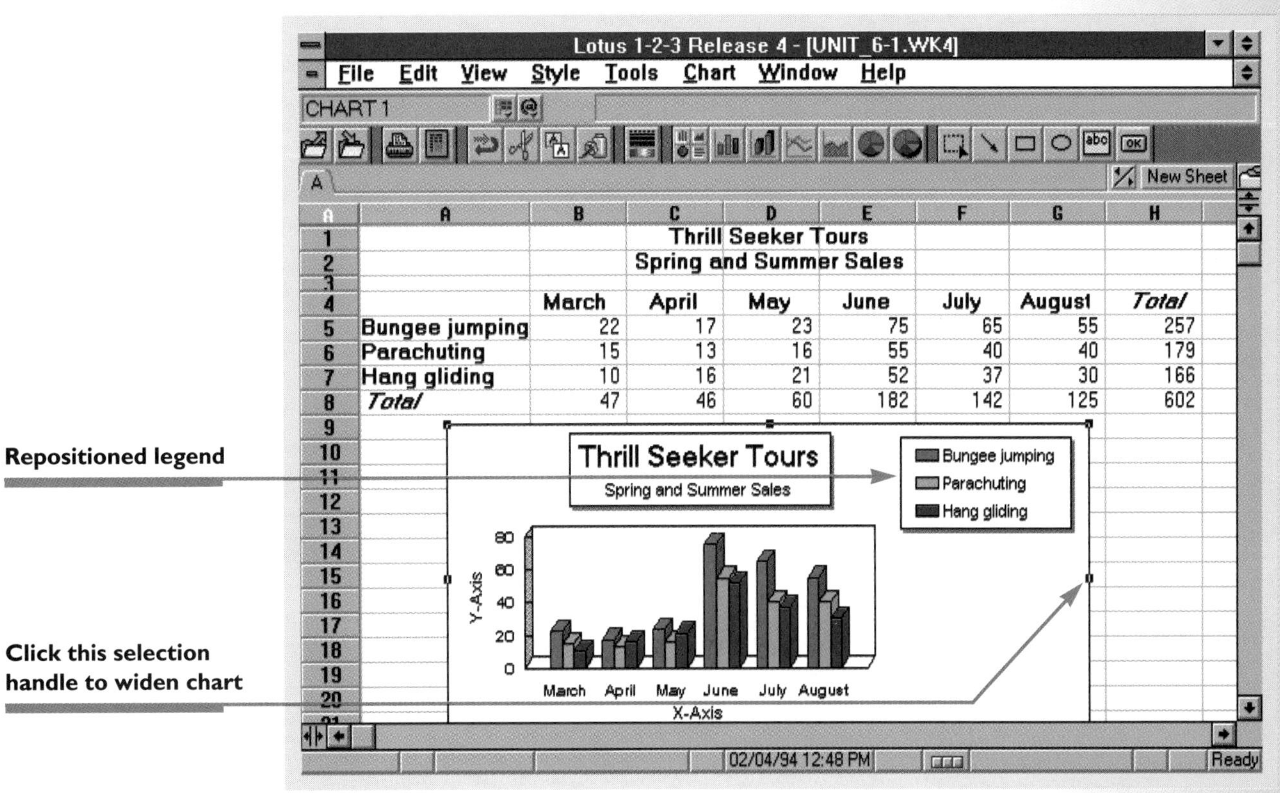

Repositioned legend

Click this selection handle to widen chart

Using Cut and Paste to move a chart

You can also move a chart by cutting it, clicking in the cell where the chart will begin, and pasting the chart. You can use either the Cut and Paste commands from the Edit menu or the Cut SmartIcon and the Paste SmartIcon.

Enhancing a chart

There are many ways to enhance a chart to make it easier to read and understand. You can create titles for the x-axis and y-axis, add graphics, change the formatting of your title, or add arrows and text annotations to highlight information. ▶ Felicia wants to improve the appearance of her chart by creating titles for the x-axis and y-axis. She also wants to add a text annotation and an arrow to highlight the June sales increase.

1   Make sure your worksheet called THRILLS.WK4 is still open and that the bar chart is selected

2   Click **Chart** in the menu bar, then click **Axis**, then click **Y-Axis**
The Y-Axis dialog box displays as shown in Figure 6-8.

3   In the Axis title text box, type **Number of tours sold** then click **OK**
The words "Number of tours sold" appears to the left of the tour numbers.

4   Click **Chart** in the menu bar, then click **Axis**, then click **X-Axis** on the Chart submenu
The X-Axis dialog box displays.

5   In the X Axis title text box, type **Months**, then click **OK**
The word "Months" displays below the month labels. Felicia now wants to highlight the increase in June sales by creating an annotation that says "After TV ads" and then drawing an arrow that points to the top of the June data series. To create her annotation, she uses the Headings dialog box.

6   Click **Chart** on the menu bar, then click **Headings...**
The Headings dialog box opens, as shown in Figure 6-9. You use this dialog box to add a title for your chart if it doesn't have one, and to add text annotations.

7   In the Notes Line 1 text box, type **After TV ads**, then click **Left**, then click **OK**
See Figure 6-9. The note "After TV ads" appears in a text box at the bottom of the chart. Felicia needs to move the text box next to the June data series.

8   Click the "After TV ads" text box to select it and drag it up to the left of the June data series, as shown in Figure 6-10
Now she needs to draw an arrow from the text box to the top of the June Bungee jump data marker.

9   Click the **Arrow SmartIcon** ⬉, then click the right edge of the text box containing "After TV ads," then drag to the top of the June data series, then release the mouse button
Notice that the pointer traces an outline of the arrow as you drag. This might take you a few tries to achieve, because the arrow is a little difficult to handle at first. If you need to delete the arrow and start again, just click the arrow to select it, then press [Del]. Compare your chart to Figure 6-10, then continue to the next lesson, keeping this worksheet open.

FIGURE 6-8:
Y-Axis dialog box

Type desired Y-axis
name here

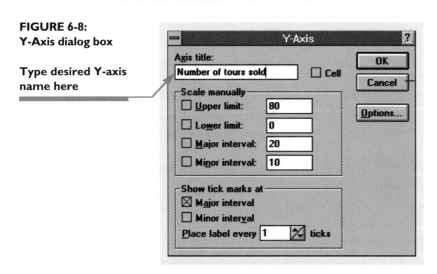

FIGURE 6-9:
Headings dialog box

Type text for chart
annotation here

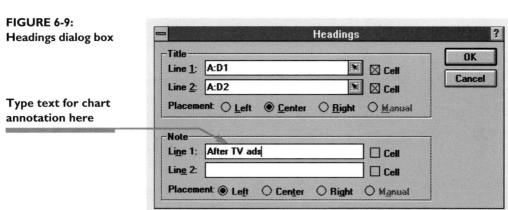

FIGURE 6-10:
**Completed chart with
named x- and y-axes,
text annotation, and
arrow**

Text annotation and
arrow

Named y-axis

Named x-axis

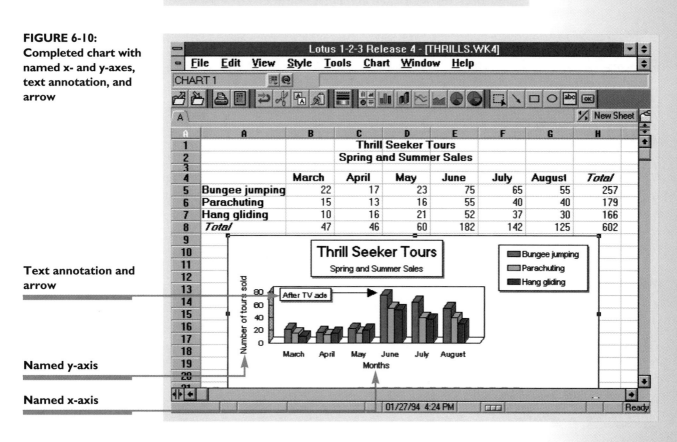

Printing charts

After you complete a chart to your satisfaction, you will most likely want to print it. You can print a chart by itself, or as part of the worksheet. ▶ Felicia is now satisfied with her chart and wants to print it for the upcoming sales meeting. She is going to print both the worksheet and the chart together, so that the sales force will see the actual sales numbers for each tour type.

S̶TEPS

1 Make sure the worksheet THRILLS.WK4 is still open

2 Click the **Print SmartIcon**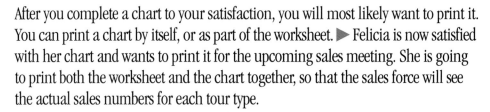
The print dialog box displays, as shown in Figure 6-11, presenting you with many options for printing your chart and/or worksheet. The options in this dialog box let print either the worksheet and chart together, or a selected range from the worksheet, or the chart by itself. Felicia wants to print both the worksheet and chart together.

3 In the Print box, click **Current worksheet**
If Felicia only wanted to print the chart, she could click the Selected chart radio button in the Print box.

4 Click **Preview**
A reduced view of the worksheet and chart displays in the Print Preview window, as shown in Figure 6-12. Felicia is satisfied with the way it looks and chooses to print it.

5 Click the **Print SmartIcon** in the Print Preview window, then click **OK** in the Print dialog box
Your printed report should look like the image displayed in the Print Preview window.

6 Click the **Save File SmartIcon** , then click **File** on the menu bar, then click **Close**
Your worksheet and chart close, with all changes saved to the file.

FIGURE 6-11: Print dialog box

When selected both worksheet and chart print

When selected, only chart prints

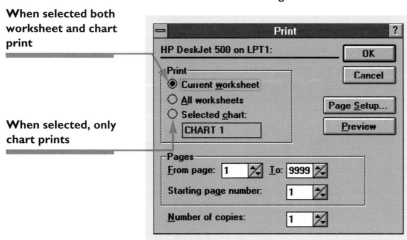

FIGURE 6-12: Chart and worksheet in the Print Preview window

Print SmartIcon

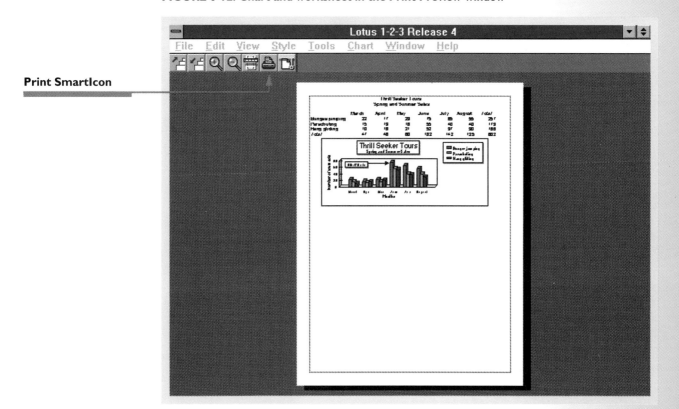

QUICK **TIP**

You can print charts and worksheets on transparencies for use on an overhead projector.■

CONCEPTSREVIEW

Label each of the Lotus 1-2-3 chart parts shown in Figure 6-14

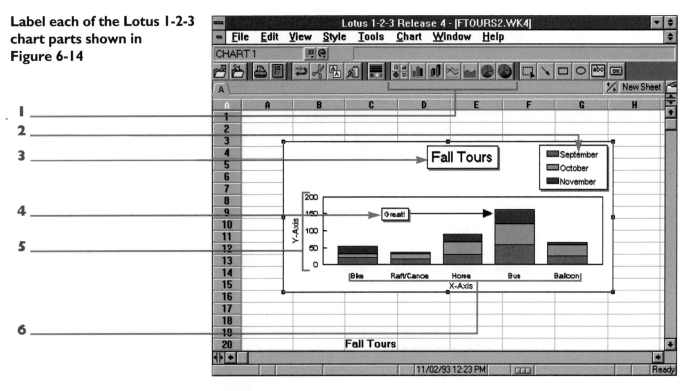

FIGURE 6-14

Select the best answer from the list of choices.

7 Use a pie chart when you want to show:

a. Trends over a period of time

b. Comparisons between data

c. Relationship of parts to a whole

d. Patterns between sets of data

8 The box that identifies data plotted on a chart is a:

a. Data series

b. Plot

c. Legend

d. Range

9 What is the term for a row or column that Lotus 1-2-3 plots on a chart?

a. Range address

b. Axis titles

c. Chart orientation

d. Data series

10 Which of the following charts is most effective for showing trends over time?

a. Line chart

b. Bar chart

c. Pie chart

d. Area chart

11 The first step to creating a chart is to:

a. Choose Chart from the Tools menu

b. Select a cell

c. Select a range

d. Choose Add-in from the Tools menu

12 To print a chart only, you need to:

a. Choose Print entire worksheet

b. Choose All worksheets

c. Select the chart, then choose Print

d. Choose Print Chart in Print Preview

APPLICATIONSREVIEW

I Create a distribution report.

    a. Open a new worksheet and use the Save As command to save it as SOFTWARE to your Student Disk.

    b. Enter the information from Table 6-5 in your worksheet.

TABLE 6-5

	Lotus 1-2-3	Microsoft Word	WordPerfect	PageMaker
Accounting	10	1	9	0
Marketing	2	9	0	6
Engineering	12	5	7	1
Personnel	2	2	2	1
Production	6	3	4	0

    c. Save your work.

2 Create a bar chart in the existing worksheet.

    a. Select all the entered information.

    b. Click Tools on the menu bar, then click Chart. Notice that the mouse pointer changes to a small chart symbol.

    c. Click the location in the worksheet where you want to insert the chart. Lotus 1-2-3 creates a default bar chart and displays it in your worksheet.

    d. Drag the right selection handle of the chart to widen it.

    e. Save your work.

3 Change the chart type in the existing worksheet.

    a. Select the chart by clicking on it. Notice that the Range menu changes to Chart.

    b. Click Chart in the menu bar, then click Type. The Type dialog box displays.

    c. Select 3-D Bar in the Types list box.

    d. Click the last sample chart, then click OK.

    e. Save your work.

4 Add an arrow to current chart.

    a. Click the Arrow SmartIcon.

    b. Click about 1" above the Personnel bar, drag down to the top of the bar, then release the mouse button. The arrow displays.

    c. Save your work.

5 Add titles to the current chart.

    a. Select the chart.

    b. Click Chart on the menu bar, then click Headings. The Headings dialog box displays.

    c. Type Software Distribution by Department in Line 1 of the Title box, then select Center placement.

    d. Type Need More Computers in Line 1 of the Note box, then click OK.

    e. Drag the note, Need More Computers, to the start of the arrow.

    f. Save your work.

6 Add axis headings to the current chart.

    a. Select the chart.

    b. Click Chart on the menu bar, then click Axis, then select X-Axis.

    c. Type Department in the Axis title text box, then click OK.

    d. Click Chart on the menu bar, then click Axis, then select Y-Axis.

    e. Type Number of Installed Packages, then click OK.

    f. Save your work.

7 Add a legend and use color in the current chart.

    a. Select the chart.

    b. Click Chart on the menu bar, then click Legend.

    c. Select Below plot in the Legend entry text box, then click OK.

    d. Click Style on the menu bar, then click Lines & Color.

    e. Choose a new Background color that you like.

    f. Choose a new Pattern.

    g. Choose a new Pattern color, then click OK.

    h. Change the colors and patterns for the labels Microsoft Word, WordPerfect, and PageMaker.

8 Preview and print the current chart.

    a. Click the Preview SmartIcon. The Print Preview dialog box displays.

    b. Click Current Worksheet, then click OK. Look at the previewed image, then click the Print SmartIcon at the top of the preview window.

    c. Now use the Print SmartIcon to print the chart only.

    d. Save your work.

INDEPENDENT
CHALLENGE

Y ou are the operations manager for the Springfield Municipal Recycling Center. The Marketing Department needs some information for a brochure that will advertise a new curbside recycling program. You need to create charts that show:

- How much of each type of recycled material Springfield collected in 1992 and what percentage of the whole each type represents. The center collects newspaper, plastics, and glass.

- The yearly increases in the total amounts of recycled materials the center has collected since its inception three years ago. Springfield has experienced a 30% annual increase in collections.

To complete this independent challenge:

1 Prepare a worksheet plan that states your goal, lists the worksheet data you'll need, and identifies the formulas for any calculations.

2 Sketch a sample worksheet on a piece of paper, describing how you will create the charts. How will you enter the worksheet data? Which type of chart is best suited for the information you need to display? What kind of chart enhancements will be necessary?

3 Build the worksheet with your own data and save the file as RECYCLE.

4 Create all of the charts, then make the appropriate enhancements. Include chart titles, legends, and axis titles. Apply color if it helps you organize your chart information on the screen.

5 Before printing, preview the file so you know what the charts will look like. Adjust any items as needed, and print copies of each of the charts. Then print a copy of the entire worksheet. Save your work before closing the file.

6 Submit your worksheet plan, preliminary sketches, and the final worksheet printouts.

UNIT 7

Working WITH DATABASES

Now that you know how to build a worksheet and perform calculations, you are ready to use one of Lotus 1-2-3's more powerful features — the database. A **database** is an organized collection of related information. A telephone book, a card catalog, and a list of company employees are all databases. Companies that distribute mass mailings and banks that manage customer accounts both rely on computer databases. ▶ Creating a database in Lotus 1-2-3 lets you organize and manage information you've gathered. Managing information gives you the ability to quickly find the data you need to work efficiently on projects or use in reports and charts. In this unit, you'll learn how to plan and create a database, add and delete information, and locate specific information within a database. ▶ The All Outdoors Tour and Travel Company uses databases for mailing lists and inventory. Elizabeth Howard, from the Tour Department, needs to build and manage a database containing information about tour customers. ▶

Planning a database

When planning a database, you need to think about the information the database will contain and how you will work with the various pieces of information. To locate specific information in a database, you need to create a field for it. **Fields** are set up as labeled columns in the database, and they describe the information that each record might contain. For example, if you want to be able to create mailing labels that would print in zip code order, you would need to create a field for the zip code. Each group of fields is a record. **Records** are set up as horizontal rows in the database and contain information entered in the fields. ► In Lotus 1-2-3, you use a range of a worksheet called a **database table**, to organize information into fields and records. The database table must fit on one worksheet and may contain up to 8,191 records with up to 256 fields. If you have more information, you need a database software application. ► Elizabeth Howard is responsible for coordinating tours and providing customer service.

■ Identify the purpose of the database. Ask yourself what kind of information it should contain. Table 7-1 describes the elements that make up a database.

Elizabeth needs to use a database to track registrations, payments, insurance waivers, and equipment rentals.

■ Plan the structure of the database. Determine the fields that will make up a record.

Elizabeth looks at the records kept on cards. Each customer in her database will have a record. These fields will correspond to the information on the cards shown in Figure 7-1.

■ Write down the names of the fields.

Elizabeth writes down the names of the fields on a card, as shown on the middle card in Figure 7-1.

■ Determine any special number formatting that will be required in the database. Most databases contain both text and numbers. When planning the structure of a database, you also need to consider whether any of the fields will require specific number formatting or prefixes.

Elizabeth notes that she will need to apply the following formats or use label prefixes for these fields:

tourdate	*12/31/93*
hnumber	*use label prefix*
wnumber	*use label prefix*
zip	*add prefix if zip code begins with 0*

TABLE 7-1:
Database elements

TERM	DEFINITION	EXAMPLE
Field	A single piece of information	Zip code
Record	A collection of several fields	Information about a specific customer
Database table	A collection of information organized into fields and records	Information about all customers

FIGURE 7-1: Card file representation of customer database

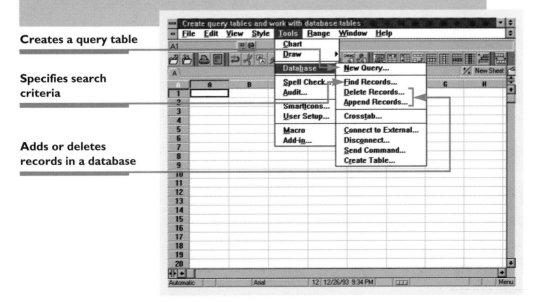

Customer information

Rodarmor, Virginia
123 Main Street
Andover, MA 01810
332-1213
935-5555

Balloon
09/15/95
Pd
Ins on file
Intermediate
no equipment

Enjoys hiking

Last name
First name
Street address
City
State
Zip
Home phone
Work phone

Tour
Tour date
Paid?
Signed insurance waiver
Skill level
Equipment needed

Comments

lastname
firstname
streetadd
city
state
zip
hphone
wphone
tour
tourdate
paystat
insure
level
equip

comments

Description of information

Fields named according to Lotus 1-2-3 guidelines

Database submenu

You can use many commands to format and calculate the contents of the database. Commands that apply only to databases are located on the Database submenu of the Tools menu, as shown in Figure 7-2.

Creates a query table

Specifies search criteria

Adds or deletes records in a database

FIGURE 7-2: Database submenu

Creating a database

Once you have planned the structure of the database, the sequence of fields, and any appropriate number formatting, you need to give the fields names that Lotus 1-2-3 will recognize. Table 7-2 lists field naming guidelines. ▶Elizabeth Howard is ready to create the database, using the field names listed on her handwritten cards. She will also select the range that the database will occupy on the worksheet.

1 **Make sure you have a blank, untitled worksheet on your screen**
If you have another worksheet currently open, click **File** on the menu bar, then click **New**.

It is a good idea to devote an entire worksheet to your database table.

2 **Beginning in cell A1 and moving horizontally, type each field name, as shown in the far right card of Figure 7-1 on page 115, into a separate cell**
Always put field names in the first row of the database table. When you finish entering all the field names continue to step 3, where you will enter records.

3 **Type the information from Figure 7-3 in the rows of cells immediately below the field names, making sure to use a label prefix such as " or ' for zip codes beginning with 0 and all phone numbers**
The data appears in columns organized by field name. Do not leave any blank rows.

Now Elizabeth wants to adjust the column widths so that each column is as wide as its longest entry.

4 **Select the range A1..O4, click Style on the menu bar, click Column Width, click Fit widest entry, then click OK**
Compare your screen with Figure 7-4.

Elizabeth is satisfied for now that her database is well designed, and that future data entry will be easy. She saves and closes the database

5 **Save your database table as DATABAS, then close the worksheet**

TABLE 7-2:
Field naming guidelines

SUBJECT	EXPLANATION
Use labels to name fields	Numbers and formulas can be interpreted as parts of formulas
Do not use duplicate field names	Duplicate field names can cause information to be incorrectly entered and sorted
Do not use punctuation or spaces	You may not use commas, periods, colons, tildes, number signs, hyphens, spaces, or +, −, *, /
Use descriptive names	Avoid names that look like cell addresses, such as Q3
Use a label prefix in a field name that starts with a number or non-alphabetic character	You must use a prefix such as ', ", or ^ for Lotus 1-2-3 to correctly recognize the field name as a label

FIGURE 7-3: Cards with customer information

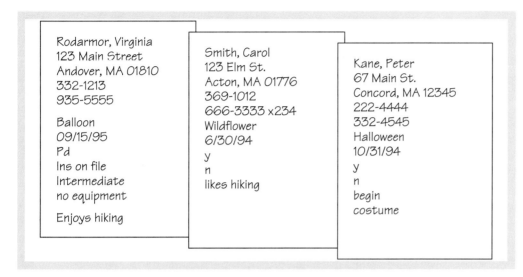

FIGURE 7-4: Database table with unsorted records

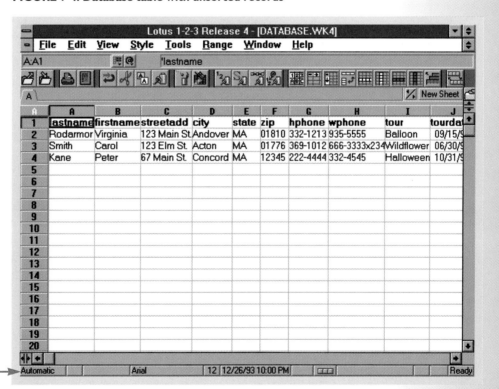

Format box

Maintaining the quality of information in a database

To protect the information, make sure that the data is entered in the correct fields. As a general rule, it's best to copy information that will be used in formulas to another worksheet. This protects the database from accidental changes.

Appending and deleting records

As you use a database, you need to keep it up to date by adding or removing records that are no longer needed. ▶ Records that will be added have to be organized in the same way as the database. Field names must be identical. Use the Append Records command on the Database submenu to tell the computer which records to add to the database. ▶ To remove records, use the Delete Records command on the Database submenu. You can tell Lotus 1-2-3 to delete all records that have something in common, such as a type of product. Specifying information in this way is called **setting criteria**. ▶ Elizabeth Howard needs to append new customer records that were typed in at the bottom of the database and to delete all records referring to the discontinued Balloon tours.

1 Open the worksheet UNIT_7-1.WK4, then save it as DATABAS2

2 Select the range **A16..O25**, click **Tools** on the menu bar, click **Database**, then click **Append Records**
The current selected range displays in the Append records from text box, as shown in Figure 7-5. You must select the field labels of the records to be appended.

The pointer changes to a 🖑, indicating that you can now specify the range of the database table.

3 Leaving the Append dialog box open, select the range **A1..O4** then click **OK**
The range of the existing database displays in the To database table text box.

The additional set of records is now included in the database. A list of the records that were appended remains below the database. You can delete this list now.

4 Select the range **A16..O25** then press **[Del]**
Elizabeth decides to delete all records that contain a reference to Balloon tours.

5 Select the range **A1..O13**, click **Tools** on the menu bar, click **Database**, then click **Delete records**
The Delete dialog box displays, as shown in Figure 7-6. You are now ready to set the criteria.

6 Click the **Field list arrow**, scroll down the list, then click **tour**
The operator symbol = indicates that the field tour will contain the specified criteria.

7 Click the **Value list arrow**, then choose **Balloon** from the list
The criteria for deleting records are displayed in the Criteria box. Tour = Balloon means that all records with Balloon in the tour field will be deleted. You could continue to apply criteria to further specify the records you want to delete.

8 Click **OK** and scroll through the database
Two records were deleted. If you ever delete records accidentally, use the Undo command or close the file without saving.

All records relating to balloon tours have been removed from the database.

9 Click the **Save File SmartIcon** to save your work, then close the file

FIGURE 7-5: Database table with Append Records dialog box

Database table

Records to be appended

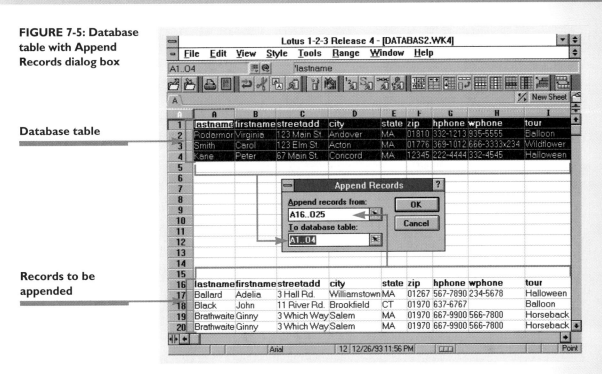

FIGURE 7-6: Database table with Delete Records dialog box

Selected range of database

Click to show list of field names

Click to show list of operator symbols

Click to display list of field contents

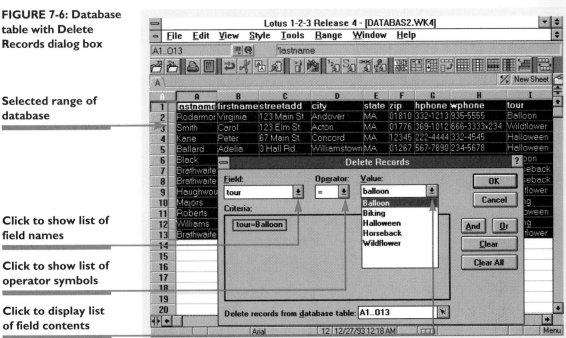

TROUBLE?

When appending data to a database, Lotus 1-2-3 ignores text formatting and treats the information as a calculation.■

Sorting records

When you add information to a database, you usually add records to the end of the database table. This means that records sharing common information may be separated and hard to view at the same time. **Sorting** allows you to rearrange the way the information in the database table displays in a way that is most useful to you. When you sort a database, you must select the entire database table *except* the field names, or the information in the database may be damaged. It's a good idea to make a back-up of your database before you sort the records. ▶ You can sort an entire database table or a selected range of a worksheet. Sorted information can be arranged in **ascending** order, that is, the smallest value appears at the top or in **descending** order, in which the largest value appears at the top. Table 7-3 provides examples of ascending and descending sorting. A cell in a range becomes the sort key. It is possible to specify different sort keys and sort the same database in other ways. For example, a sales manager can sort the same records by region, by product, and by sales representative to create different reports. ▶ Elizabeth wants to sort the records by the lastname and tour fields. First she wants to number the records so she can keep track of their original order.

1 Open the worksheet UNIT_7-2.WK4, then save it as DATABAS3

2 Select all the records in the database table (A2..O11), then pull down the **Range menu** and choose **Sort**
   Lotus 1-2-3 displays the Sort dialog box, as shown in Figure 7-7.

3 Click any cell in column **A**, check that **Ascending** is selected, then click **OK**
   The Sort key should list one cell only. The data table is sorted alphabetically by last name and the record number sequence has changed, as shown in Figure 7-8.

4 Select A2..O11, (it should be selected already) click **Range** on the menu bar, click **Sort**, then click **Reset**
   All ranges used to sort are deleted from the Sort dialog box.

5 With the Sort dialog box open, click any cell in the tour column (coumn I) click **Ascending**, then click **OK**
   As you make your selection, the mode indicator displays the word Point. The records are now sorted by tour, as shown in Figure 7-9.

   You can also specify additional sort keys, in the Sort dialog box and perform a sort within a sort. Save your changes but do not close your worksheet.

6 Save your changes, keep the worksheet open, and continue to the next lesson

FIGURE 7-7: The Sort dialog box

Sort key displays here

Additional sort keys might display here

Click to add a sort key

Click to restore previous sort criteria

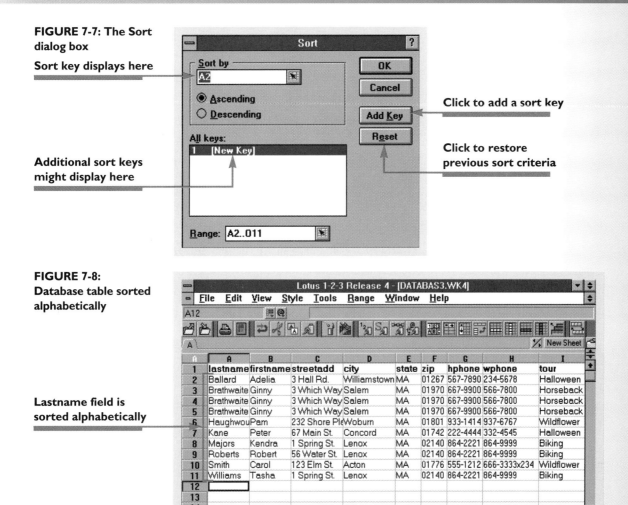

FIGURE 7-8: Database table sorted alphabetically

Lastname field is sorted alphabetically

FIGURE 7-9: Database table sorted by tour type

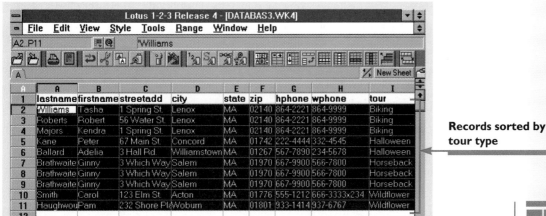

Records sorted by tour type

TABLE 7-3: Sort options

OPTION	EXAMPLE
Ascending	7,8,9 or A,B,C
Descending	9,8,7 or C,B,A

TROUBLE?

Use the Reset button in the Sort dialog box to clear unwanted ranges that may cause the "Key column outside of Sort range" warning.■

Finding records

You often need to locate specific information in a database. In Unit 4, you learned about the Find & Replace command located on the Edit menu which can find each occurrence of the criteria you want to locate. The Find Records command located on the Database submenu allows you to tell Lotus 1-2-3 which information to locate. The Find Records command finds and highlights all records with specific search criteria at the same time. ▶ You can refine your searches of field contents by using operator symbols. Operator symbols give you the ability to focus your search within a field. For example, by using the mathematical symbol for greater than (>) and specifying the value $10,000, you could exclude all amounts under $10,000 from a search. Table 7-4 explains the different operator symbols available in the Find Records dialog box. ▶ Elizabeth Howard wants to find all the customers who signed up for horseback tours and all the customers who signed up for tours before July 30, 1994.

1 Select the range **A1..O11**, then click **Tools** on the menu bar, then click **Database**, then click **Find Records**
The Find Records dialog box displays on the screen, as shown in Figure 7-10. Now Elizabeth will specify the field name which is tour.

2 Click the **Field list arrow**, scroll down the list, then click **tour**
Now Elizabeth needs to specify that the kind of tour she wants to identify is horseback.

3 Click the **Value list arrow**, click **Horseback**, then click **OK**
The criteria display in the Criteria list box. Once you click OK, all records containing Horseback are highlighted. Notice that three records are highlighted, all for Ginny Braithwaite. This is because Ginny signed up for horseback tours on three different dates. Now Elizabeth wants to locate tours that occurred before the date 7/30/94.

4 Select the range **A1..O11**, click **Tools** on the menu bar, click **Database**, then click **Find Records**

5 Click the **Field list arrow**, then click **tourdate**
Now Elizabeth will set the criteria for tours before 7/30/94.

6 Click the **operator list arrow**, click the less than symbol **(<)**, select the contents of the Value box and type **7/30/94**, then click **OK**
Lotus 1-2-3 highlights all tours that occurred before 7/30/94. Compare your screen with Figure 7-11. Notice that the previous search results are no longer highlighted.

7 Click the **Save File SmartIcon** 💾 to save your changes
Keep the worksheet open and continue to the next lesson.

FIGURE 7-10: Find Records dialog box

Click to display list of fields

Click to display list of operator symbols

Click to display list of field contents

Specify range to search

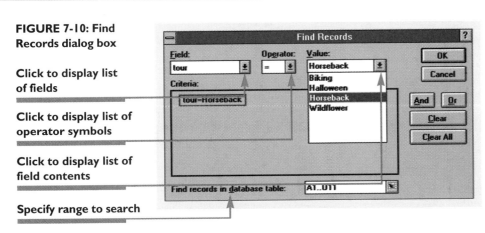

FIGURE 7-11: Database table with highlighted search results

Highlighted tours before 7/30/94

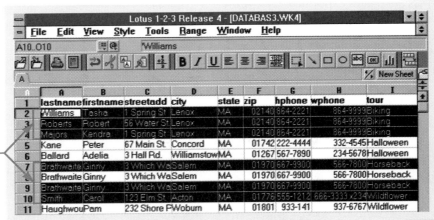

Using wildcard symbols

Wildcard symbols enable you to search records by specifying only part of the search criteria. To search for last names beginning with Mo, use Mo* as the search criteria. Lotus 1-2-3 would locate last names such as: Molea, Montgomery, Morris, and Morrison.

To search for records when you are not sure of the exact spelling, use the ? wildcard. Enter All?n to find Allan, Allyn, and Allen.

TABLE 7-4: Operator symbols in the Find Records dialog box

SYMBOL	EXPLANATION
=	The specified field is equal to this value
<	The specified field is less than this value
>	The specified field is greater than this value
<=	The specified field is less than or equal to this value
>=	The specified field is greater than or equal to this value
<>	The specified field is not equal to this value

QUICK **TIP**

To change from the And to the Or search option, click one of the criteria in the Criteria list box and drag it to the right.■

Finding records with multiple search criteria

Each time you perform a search, Lotus 1-2-3 highlights the records matching each different set of criteria. To locate and highlight records that have more than one field in common, you need to use multiple search criteria. ▶ You can also specify whether search criteria should be linked. If you click And in the Find Records dialog box, Lotus 1-2-3 would locate only those customers who signed up for horseback tours *and* who took the tour before 7/30/94. If you click Or, Lotus 1-2-3 would highlight all records with tours that occurred before 7/30/94 in addition to all horseback tours. ▶ Elizabeth needs to locate all customers who signed up for horseback tours before 7/30/94.

1 Select the range **A1..O11**, then click **Tools** on the menu bar, then click **Database** then click **Find Records**
   The Find Records dialog box displays. Now Elizabeth will specify the search criteria.

2 Click the **Field list arrow**, then click **Tour**
   Elizabeth will specify **Horseback** in the Value list box.

3 Click the **Value list arrow**, then click **Horseback**
   The criteria are listed in the criteria box. Now Elizabeth will specify for Lotus 1-2-3 to find only Horseback tours that occurred before 7/30/94. She will use the And button.

4 Click **And**, click the **Field list arrow**, then choose **tourdate**

5 Click the **Operator list box down arrow**, click <, select the contents of the Value box and type **7/30/94** in the value box, then click **OK**
   The criteria are listed in the Find Records dialog box, as shown in Figure 7-12. When you click OK, Lotus 1-2-3 highlights two records, both for Ginny Braithwarte. Ginny took the Horseback tours on 6/25/94 and 5/25/94.

   If Elizabeth wanted to find all records that either occurred before 7/30/94 or were horseback tours, she would have followed the same steps, above, but would have used the Or button in step 4 instead of the And button.

6 Save your worksheet and close the file

FIGURE 7-12: Find Records dialog box with multiple search criteria

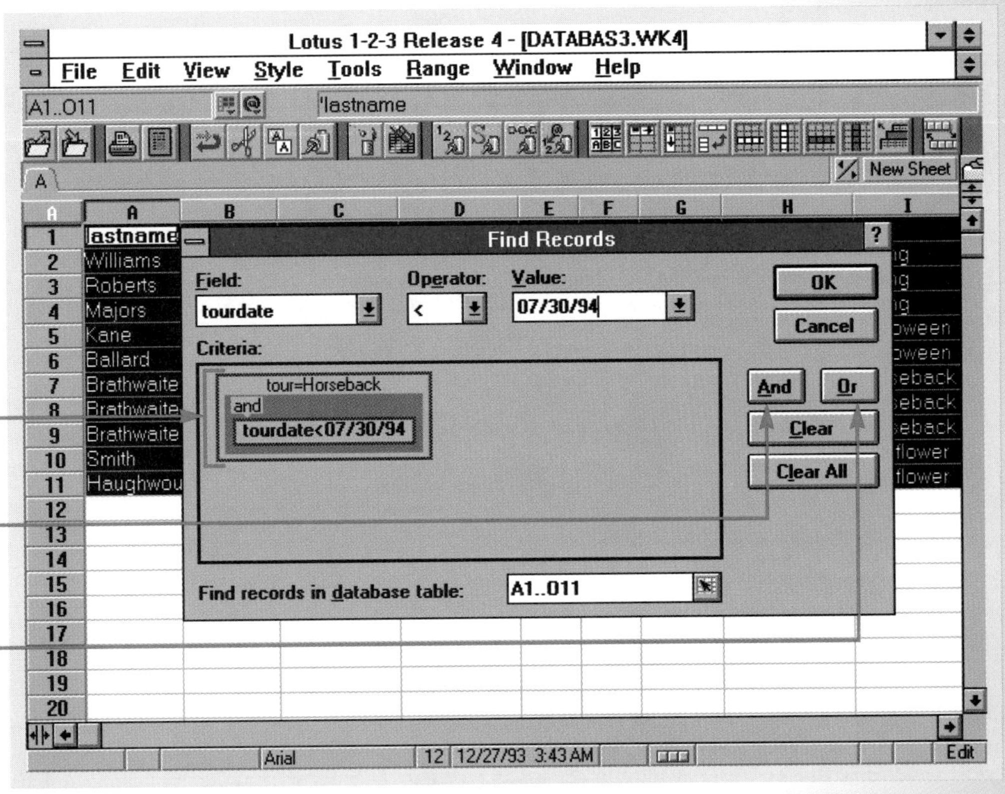

"And" indicates that the criteria are linked

Click to link search criteria

Click to simultaneously find several sets of search criteria

Searching a database with a query table

You can also locate information in database by using a query table. When you use a query table, the search criteria filters out all the information you don't need. Lotus 1-2-3 displays only the search criteria in a table outside of the database table. You can quickly organize information in a query table as reports and charts. Figure 7-13 shows a query table showing customers that are intermediates.

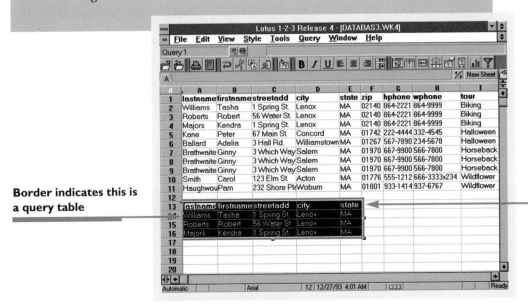

Border indicates this is a query table

These fields and their data are extracted from the database and placed in a query table

FIGURE 7-13: Query table

CONCEPTSREVIEW

Label each of the elements of the Lotus 1-2-3 database shown in Figure 7-14.

1 _____

2 _____

3 _____

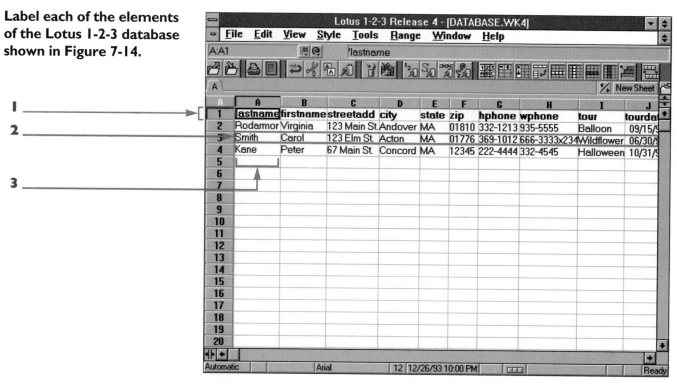

FIGURE 7-14

Match each of the statements with the term it describes.

4 To arrange records in a particular sequence

5 Organized collection of related information

6 Row in a Lotus 1-2-3 database

7 Column in a Lotus 1-2-3 database containing information related to a record

8 Label positioned at the top of the column identifying data for that field

a. Field

b. Record

c. Database

d. Sort

e. Field name

Select the best answer from the list of choices.

9 Which of the following Lotus 1-2-3 sorting options do you use to sort a database of employee names in A-to-Z order?

a. Ascending

b. Absolute

c. Alphabet

d. Advanced

10 Which of the following series of numbers is in descending order?

a. 4, 5, 6, 5, 4

b. 4, 5, 6, 7, 8

c. 8, 7, 6, 5, 4

d. 4, 6, 8, 6, 4

APPLICATIONSREVIEW

1 On paper, plan and design an employee database for M.K. Electric Sales.

   a. Column A will contain the lastname field.

   b. Column B will contain the firstname field.

   c. Column C will contain the years field.

   d. Column D will contain the position field.

   e. Column E will contain the pension field.

   f. Column F will contain the union field.

2 Build the employee database.

   a. Type the title M.K. Electric Sales Employees at the top of the worksheet.

   b. Type the field names in the appropriate columns, using your planning sketch from exercise 1.

   c. Enter the records in the appropriate fields using the information in Table 7-5.

TABLE 7-5

Last Name	First Name	Years	Position	Pension	Union
Smith-Hill	Janice	8	Office Manager	Y	N
Doolan	Mark	3	Customer Service	N	N
Coleman	Steve	4	Senior Installer	N	Y
Quinn	Jamie	7	Junior Installer	N	Y
Rabinowicz	Sarah	11	Field Manager	Y	Y

   d. Save the database as EMPLOYEE to your Student Disk.

3 Make formatting changes to the current database.

   a. Center-align the entries in the Pension and Union columns.

   b. Adjust the column widths of the lastname and position fields to make the data readable.

   c. Save and print the worksheet.

4 Add records to the current database.

   a. Four rows below the last record in the database table, retype the field names from your database, then add a new record for David Gitano, a newly hired junior installer at M.K. Electric Sales. David is not eligible for the employee pension, but he is a member of the union.

   b. In the row immediately below the Gitano entry, add a new record for George Worley, the company's new office assistant. George is not eligible for the employee pension, and he is not a union member.

   c. Select the range containing the records that you want to add to the employee database. Make sure you include the field names that you retyped.

   d. Click Tools on the menu bar then click Database.

   e. Click Append Records from the Database submenu. The Append Records dialog box displays.

   f. Enter the range of the existing database in the To database table text box, then click OK. Lotus 1-2-3 appends the new employee records to the end of the database.

5 Find records of pension-eligible employees in the current database.

   a. Select the database.

   b. Click Tools on the menu bar, then click Database

   c. Click Find Records from the Database submenu. The Find Records dialog box displays.

   d. Click Pension from the Field list box. This is the field in which Lotus 1-2-3 will search for information.

   e. Click = in the Operator list box.

   f. Click Y in the Value list box, then click OK. Lotus 1-2-3 highlights all the records that match your criteria.

6 Sort the current database alphabetically by last name.

   a. Specify the range of records in the database table. Make sure you include only the records, not the field names.

   b. Click Range in the menu bar then click Sort. The Sort dialog box displays.

   c. In the Sort by text box, enter one cell in the appropriate column.

   d. Click Ascending in the options underneath the Sort by text box, then click OK. Lotus 1-2-3 sorts the specified range in A-to-Z order.

   e. Save and print the sorted worksheet.

INDEPENDENTCHALLENGE

You are the program director of Blair Cinema, an independent movie house that specializes in foreign and specialty films. One of your responsibilities is to compile a list of "movie buff" data about the actresses who will be featured in an upcoming film festival, "Women in Film: Past and Present." The two-week event will honor Hollywood legends such as Katharine Hepburn and Joan Crawford, and will showcase contemporary stars such as Susan Sarandon and Mary McDonnell.

Plan and build a database of information about 10 movie actresses to be featured in the film festival. Enter your own data (based on what you know about your own movie favorites), but make sure you include at least the following database fields:

- Genre—Is the actress known primarily as a comic or dramatic actress?

- Films—In approximately how many films has the actress appeared?

- Most popular—For what film is the actress best known?

- Oscar—Has the actress won an Academy Award for her performance in a film?

To complete this independent challenge:

1 Prepare a database plan that states your goal, lists the worksheet data you'll need, and identifies the database table elements.

2 Sketch a sample worksheet on a piece of paper, indicating how the database table should be built. Which actresses will you include? What information should go in the columns? In the rows? Which of the data fields will be formatted as labels? As values? If you have trouble compiling information about actresses, check the movie section of your local newspaper for ideas.

3 Build the worksheet by entering the worksheet title and field names first, then entering the records. Remember you are creating and entering your own movie data. Save the worksheet as CINEMA.

4 Make formatting changes to the database, as needed. For example, you may need to adjust the column widths to make the data more readable. Also, remember to check your spelling.

5 Sort the database alphabetically by last name. Before printing, preview the file so you know what the worksheet will look like. Adjust any items as needed, and print a copy. Next, sort the database by genre so you can easily see how many comedic actresses and how many dramatic actresses are represented in the festival. Preview the worksheet, then print it. Save your work before closing the file.

6 Submit your database plan, preliminary sketches, and the final worksheet printouts.

UNIT 8

OBJECTIVES

▶ Add worksheet windows to a file

▶ View and move between worksheet windows

▶ Copy data from one worksheet window to another

▶ Open multiple worksheet files

▶ Copy data and move between open worksheet files

Using
MULTIPLE WORKSHEETS AND FILES

You can create a file that contains more than one worksheet window. This feature allows you to organize related information in one file. In this unit you will learn how to add additional worksheet windows to a file, how to view the different worksheet windows, and how to copy information from one worksheet window to another. ▶ With Lotus 1-2-3, you also have the option of working with more than one open worksheet file. With multiple open files, you can copy and paste labels, figures, and formulas from one file to another. In this unit, you will also learn how to open more than one worksheet file, and how to copy data from one file to another. ▶ Sean Drucker from the Accounting Department of the All Outdoors Tour and Travel Company wants to create a file that contains several worksheet windows. He also needs to review several files that document expenses. ▶

Adding worksheet windows to a file

Additional worksheet windows can be used to organize related information or groups of information that need to be analyzed in reports, charts, or databases. Each worksheet window is identified by a worksheet tab. To name worksheet windows, double-click the worksheet tab, type the name, then press[Enter]. If you leave the worksheet windows unnamed, Lotus 1-2-3 identifies the worksheet windows with the letters of the alphabet. ▶ There are several ways to add worksheet windows to a file. To add one worksheet at a time, click the New Sheet button under the SmartIcon palette. With the Insert command on the Edit menu, you can create more than one worksheet window at a time. ▶ Sean Drucker has a worksheet used to report on company-wide expenses. He wants to add worksheet windows to this file to track departmental and overhead expenses.

STEPS

1   Click **File** on the menu bar, then click **New**, then save the file as EXPENSES

2   Double-click **worksheet tab A** located below the title bar
The worksheet tab looks like the tab on a file folder. When you double-click the worksheet tab, it becomes wider and displays a blinking cursor. You are ready to name the first tab.

3   Type the name **Company Expense** then press **[Enter]**
Company Expense displays in worksheet tab A.

4   Click the **New Sheet button** in the upper-right corner under the SmartIcon palette
Worksheet tab B displays. You are ready to name this tab.

5   Double-click **worksheet tab B**, type **Overhead**, then press **[Enter]**
Overhead displays in worksheet tab B. Now use the Insert command to add worksheet windows.

6   Click **Edit** on the menu bar, then click **Insert**
The Insert dialog box displays, as shown in Figure 8-1.

7   Click **Sheet**, type **2** in the **Quantity box**, then click **OK**
Worksheet tabs C and D display.

8   Double click **Worksheet tab C**, type **Accounting**, then press **[Enter]**

9   Double click **Worksheet tab D**, type **Marketing**, then press **[Enter]**
Compare your screen with Figure 8-2.

10   Save your changes and close the worksheet

FIGURE 8-1: Insert dialog box

Choose worksheet placement of new worksheet windows

Click these arrows to select the number of sheets

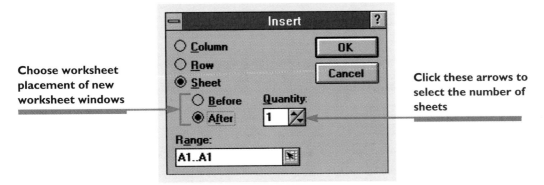

FIGURE 8-2: Worksheet with added tabs

Named worksheet tabs

Click to add new worksheet windows

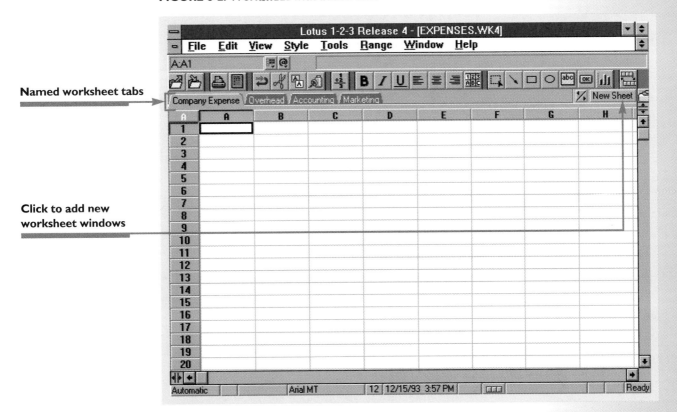

Deleting a worksheet window

To delete a worksheet window, click the worksheet tab of the window you wish to delete, click **Edit** on the menu bar, then click **Delete**. When the Delete dialog box displays, click Sheet, then click OK. Lotus 1-2-3 deletes the woksheet window from the worksheet.

QUICK TIP

Use the same cell addresses for the same type of information on each worksheet window to minimize scrolling.■

Viewing and moving between worksheet windows

Clicking each worksheet tab allows you to move from one worksheet window to another but it does not provide a convenient way to view information. With **perspective view**, you can display portions of up to three smaller worksheet windows at the same time. Lotus 1-2-3 provides several ways to move between open worksheet windows. Table 8-1 lists keyboard shortcuts for moving between open worksheet windows. ▶ Sean wants to view several expense records before he creates the report for company expenses. Sean added borders to the worksheet because he will be printing the selected areas on overhead transparencies for an upcoming meeting.

1 Open the worksheet UNIT_8-1.WK4, then save it as EXPENSE2

2 Click the **Marketing worksheet tab**
The worksheet window containing Marketing expenses moves to the front. Now click the other tabs to move to the other worksheet windows.

3 Click **View** on the menu bar, then click **Split**
The Split dialog box displays, as shown in Figure 8-3.

4 Click **Perspective**, then click **OK**
The worksheet windows display, as shown in Figure 8-4. Note that the worksheet tabs are no longer displayed. Press **[F6]** to move to another worksheet window.

5 Press **[Ctrl] [PgUp]**
The cell pointer moves up to the middle window. Press **[Ctrl] [PgUp]** again to move to the top window.

6 Press **[Ctrl] [PgDn]**
The cell pointer moves down to the middle window.

7 Press **[Ctrl] [Home]**
The cell pointer moves to A1 on the first worksheet window.

8 Click **View** on the menu bar, then click **Clear Split**
The worksheet displays normally. Save your work and continue to the next lesson without closing your worksheet.

TABLE 8-1:
Keyboard shortcuts for moving between worksheet windows

SHORTCUT	WORKSHEET WINDOW
[Ctrl] [PgUp]	Moves up a window
[Ctrl] [PgDn]	Moves down a window
[Ctrl] [Home]	Moves to A1 in the first window

FIGURE 8-3: Split dialog box

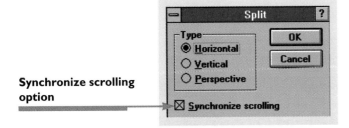

Synchronize scrolling
option

FIGURE 8-4: Multiple worksheet windows in perspective view

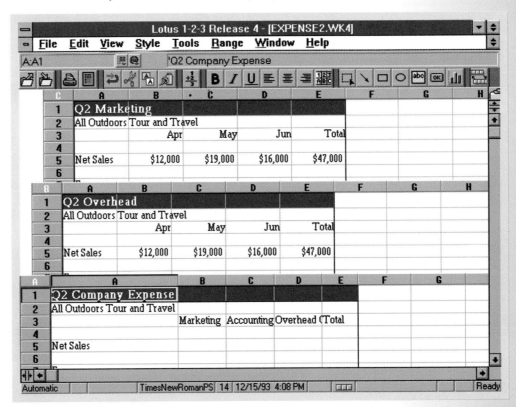

Synchronized scrolling

Choose the Synchronized scrolling option in the Split dialog box to scroll simultaneously through worksheet windows displayed in perspective view.

QUICK **TIP**

Differentiate work-
sheet windows by
using the Lines &
Color command to
assign different back-
ground colors.■

Copying data from one worksheet window to another

When you work with different worksheet windows, it's easy to copy and paste information from one worksheet window to another. First, determine if you want to copy the values or the formulas of the selected area. To paste formulas but not their results, use the Paste command from the Edit menu. To paste the value that appears as a result of a formula, use the Paste Special command on the Edit menu. ▶ To create an expense report, Sean Drucker needs to copy the values located on the other open worksheet windows to create an expense report.

STEPS

1 Click the **Marketing worksheet tab** and click cell **E8**
   You are ready to copy and paste this information to another worksheet window.

2 Click **Edit** on the menu bar, click **Copy**
   The contents of E8 is copied to the Clipboard.

3 Click the **Company Expense worksheet tab**, then click cell **B8**
   Now use the Paste Special command to copy the total appearing in cell B8.

4 Click **Edit**, on the menu bar, click **Paste Special**, click **Formulas as values**, then click **OK**
   The Paste Special dialog box is shown in Figure 8-5. The total from cell E8 on the Marketing worksheet window is copied to B8 on the Company Expense worksheet window. Using the Paste Special command, finish copying all of the salary information from the Accounting worksheet window ($24,000) and Overhead worksheet window ($6,000) into Cells C8 and D8 on the Company Expenses worksheet window. When you are done, continue to step 5.

5 Click cell **E8** in the **Company Expense worksheet window,** then click the **@function selector button,** then click **SUM**
   The @function selector drops down from the edit line.

6 Select the range **B8..D8** and press **[Enter]**
   $44,500 displays in cell E8. Sean will continue this process to create the rest of his worksheet.

7 Save your work and close the file

FIGURE 8-5: Paste Special dialog box

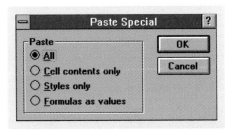

FIGURE 8-6: Worksheet with copied data

@function selector
button

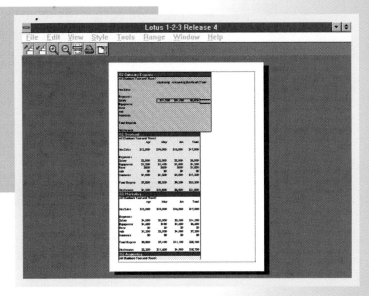

Printing multiple worksheet windows

You can print information that appears on different worksheet windows on the same page. To select cells from different worksheet windows, select data from the first cell, then hold down [Ctrl] and continue making selections. In Figure 8-7 the worksheets were given different background colors.

FIGURE 8-7: Multiple worksheet windows in Print Preview

Opening multiple worksheet files

Just as you can work with multiple windows in one file, you can also work with multiple worksheet files. It's not uncommon for individuals or departments to create their own worksheet files and then share them with others by disk or network. When each group maintains its own file, the information is more likely to be up to date and accurate. To open multiple worksheet files, pull down the File menu, choose Open, and select the filename of each file you wish to open. Use the Open command until you have opened all the files you wish to work with. Table 8-2 compares worksheet windows with worksheet files. ▶ Sean Drucker needs to review files containing the expenses that were submitted in separate files from the marketing and accounting departments.

1 Open the worksheet UNIT_8-2.WK4, then save it as MARKGEXP

2 Open the worksheet UNIT_8-3.WK4, then save it as ACCTGEXP
Two worksheet files are now open.

3 Open the worksheet UNIT_8-4.WK4, then save it as COEXPENS
Three worksheet files are open. Now you are ready to move between the open worksheet files.

4 Click **Window** on the menu bar, then click MARKGEXP.WK4
MARKGEXP.WK4 moves to the front. Now try making other selections from the Window menu.

5 Click **Window** on the menu bar, then click **Tile**
Lotus 1-2-3 resizes all the open windows so that they all display, as shown in Figure 8-8.

6 Click **Window** on the menu bar, then click **Cascade**
The worksheets are cascaded, as shown in Figure 8-9.

7 In the MARKGEXP window, click the **Maximize button** in the upper-right corner of the title bar
The window is enlarged to fill up the entire screen. Continue to the next lesson without closing the files.

TABLE 8-2: Comparison of worksheet windows and worksheet files

TYPE	FEATURES
Worksheet window	Uses worksheet tabs to visually separate information; you open only one file to access all the information
Worksheet file	Information is contained in individually named and created files, which can be opened individually with the Open command

FIGURE 8-8: Tiled worksheets

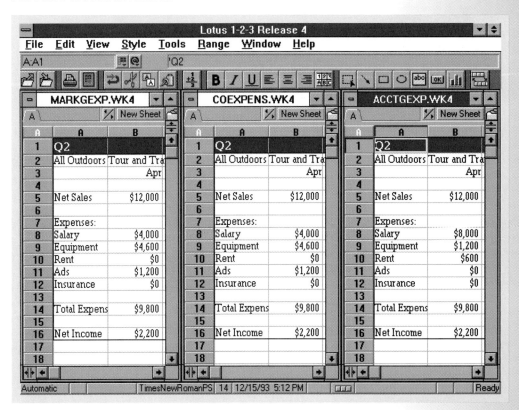

FIGURE 8-9: Cascaded worksheets

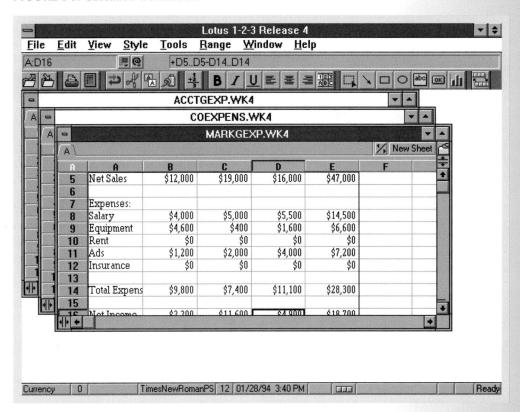

Copying data and moving between open worksheet files

When you have more than one file open, you can copy and paste information such as labels, values, and formulas from one open worksheet file to another. To make a worksheet the current one, you can click anywhere on a worksheet or click Window on the menu bar, then click the filename you want. ▶ Sean Drucker wants to copy the accounting, marketing, and overhead expenses to a new worksheet called REPORT.

1 Click **File** on the menu bar, click **New**, then save the worksheet as REPORT
You should have the following four files open at this time: REPORT.WK4, MARKGEXP.WK4, ACCTGEXP.WK4, and COEXPENS.WK4.

2 In **B6**, type the label **Marketing**, in **C6** type **Accounting**, in **D6** type **Overhead**, and in **E6** type **Total**
Now Sean will copy the Marketing totals.

3 Click **Window** on the menu bar, then click **MARKGEXP.WK4**
MARKGEXP becomes the current worksheet file.

4 In MARKGEXP, select the range **E8..E14**, then click the **Copy SmartIcon** 🔳
The Marketing totals are copied to the Clipboard. Now Sean will paste them to the REPORT worksheet using the Paste Special command.

5 Click **Window** on the menu bar, then click **REPORT.WK4**
REPORT is now the current worksheet.

6 In REPORT, click cell **B7**, click **Edit** on the menu bar, click **Paste Special**, click **Formulas as values**, then click **OK**
Marketing totals are pasted into the range B7..B13. Now, on your own, copy the Totals in range E8..E14 from the ACCTGEXP worksheet into C7..C13 of the REPORT worksheet. Then copy the Totals in the range E8..E14 in the COEXPENS worksheet into D7..D13 of the REPORT worksheet. Use the same method that you used in steps 4 and 5, above, making sure to use the Paste Special command. When you are done, compare your results with the C and D columns in Figure 8-10, then continue to step 7.

7 Click **Window** on the menu bar, then click **REPORT.WK4**
The Report worksheet displays and is now the current worksheet. Sean now has successfully copied all the data he needs from ACCTGEXP and COEXPENS. Now he will use the Sum Range SmartIcon to fill in the totals in Column E.

8 Select the range **E7..E13**, then click the Sum **Range SmartIcon** 🔳
All the totals should correctly display in the range E7..E13. Check your screen against Figure 8-10. Sean now wants to apply the currency format to the E column.

9 Select the range **E7..E13**, then click the **format box** in the Status bar, then click **Currency**
All the values should now correctly display as currency, as shown in Figure 8-10.

10 Save and close each worksheet one at a time until they are all closed

FIGURE 8-10: File with copied information

Format box

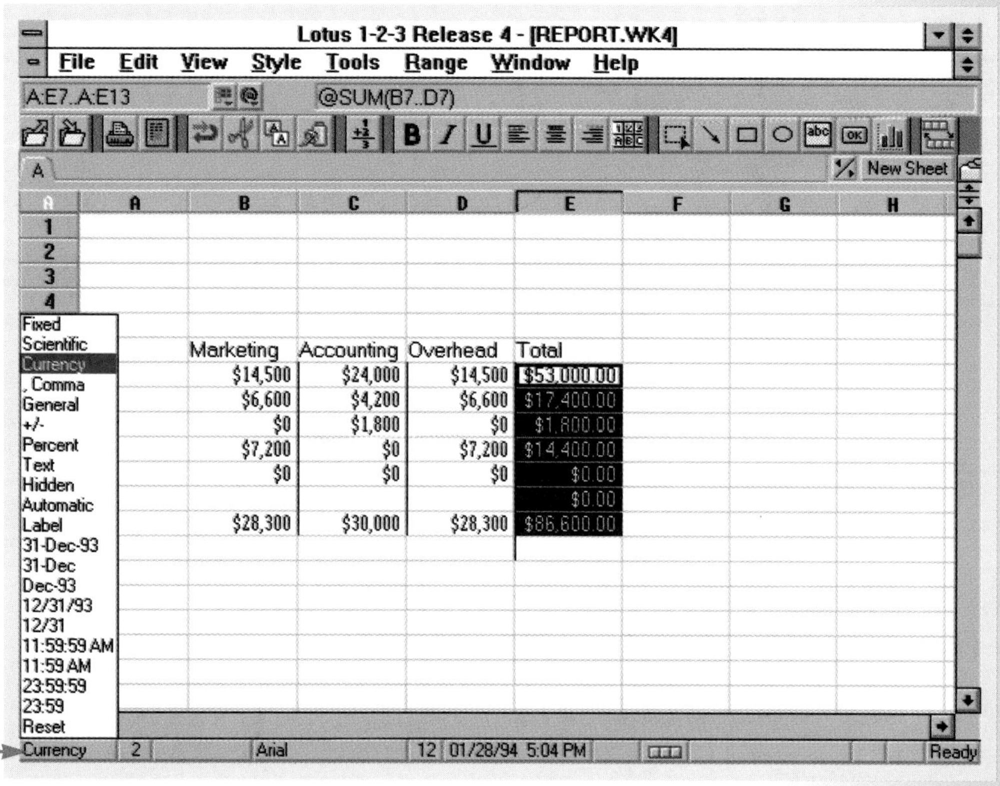

Copying a worksheet file to a worksheet window

You can copy information from a separate file to a worksheet window in another file. First, create a new worksheet window, then switch to the other worksheet and copy the information. Move to the other worksheet window and paste the information there.

QUICK **TIP**

Use the Combine option in the Open dialog box to combine the contents of two files.■

CONCEPTSREVIEW

Label each of the elements of the Lotus 1-2-3 screen shown in Figure 8-11.

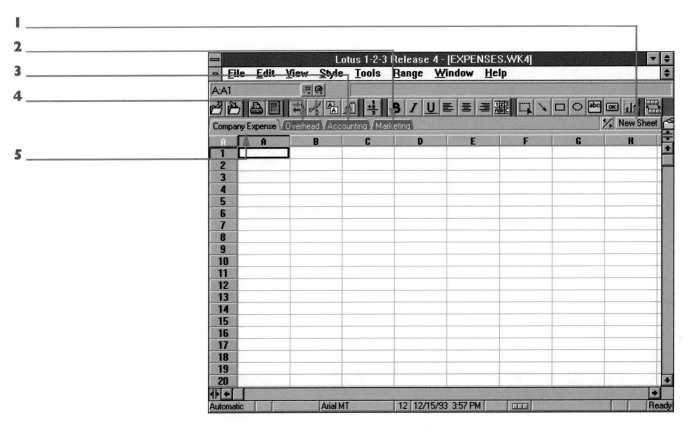

1

2

3

4

5

FIGURE 8-11

Match each of the statements with the keyboard shortcut it describes.

6 Moves the cell pointer up to the next worksheet window in an open file

7 Moves the cell pointer to cell A1 of the first sheet window in an open file

8 Moves the cell pointer to the previous sheet window in a worksheet file

    a. [Ctrl][Home]

    b. [Ctrl][PgDn]

    c. [Ctrl][PgUp]

Select the best answer from the list of choices.

9 When you work in perspective view, you can see portions of how many worksheet windows at one time?

    a. One

    b. Two

    c. Three

    d. Four

10 You can copy or move information from one worksheet file to another by placing information on the:

    a. Worksheet tab

    b. Mode indicator

    c. Contents box

    d. Clipboard

APPLICATIONS REVIEW

1 Insert new worksheet windows into a worksheet file.

a. Open a new worksheet and save it as PRACTICE to your Student Disk.

b. Type your name and today's date at the top of the worksheet.

c. Click the New Sheet button near the top right corner of the screen. A new worksheet window displays.

d. Repeat the step above to add a third worksheet window to the worksheet file.

2 View the current worksheet in perspective view.

a. Check that you have three worksheet windows displayed on your screen. If you don't see the worksheet tabs A, B, and C near the top left corner of the screen, you need to add new worksheets.

b. Click Veiw on the menu bar and click Split. The Split dialog box displays.

c. Click Perspective, then click OK. Lotus 1-2-3 displays two worksheet windows in perspective view. Now try changing back to viewing a full-screen worksheet.

d. Click View on the menu bar and click Clear Split. Lotus 1-2-3 restores the worksheet window to its original size; you can now see the worksheet tabs for the other worksheet windows.

3 Practice moving between worksheet windows.

a. Click the worksheet tab B.

b. Press [Ctrl][PgUp]. Notice that the cell pointer moves to the next sheet window. With Lotus 1-2-3, you can use either the mouse or the keyboard to move between worksheet windows in an open file.

c. Continue navigating between the open worksheet windows.

4 Delete a worksheet window from the current worksheet file.

a. Move to worksheet C by pressing [Ctrl][PgUp] or clicking the worksheet tab.

b. Click Edit on the menu bar and click Delete. The Delete dialog box displays.

c. Click Sheet in the options listed in the dialog box, then click OK. Lotus 1-2-3 deletes the worksheet window from the worksheet.

5 Open multiple worksheet files.

a. Open the CHAIRS worksheet that you created in exercise 1 of the Unit 5 Applications Review. The Country Oak Chairs quarterly sales worksheet displays.

b. Open a new worksheet and name it UPDATE. The new worksheet displays in front of the original worksheet.

c. Set up the worksheet using the data from Table 8-3.

TABLE 8-3
Country Oak Chairs, Inc.
Sales Update

Description	Price	Sold
Cottage bench	$899	645
Chaise lounge	$649	800

d. Save the worksheet.

6 View multiple worksheet files.

a. Click Window on the menu bar and click Cascade. Lotus 1-2-3 cascades the CHAIRS, UPDATE, and PRACTICE files on the screen.

b. Click Window on the menu bar and click Tile. Lotus 1-2-3 resizes the open worksheet files so that you can view parts of both files at the same time.

7 Move between open worksheet files.

a. Cascade the CHAIRS and UPDATE worksheet files.

b. Practice using the [Ctrl][PgDn] and [Ctrl][PgUp] keys to move the cell pointer from file to file.

c. Practice using the mouse to move back and forth between the two open worksheet files.

d. Press [Ctrl][Home] and watch the cell pointer move to cell A1 of the first open worksheet file.

8 Copy data between open worksheet files.

a. Move to the UPDATE worksheet file.

b. Select the range that contains the data for the two additional chairs. You don't need to select the column titles or worksheet titles.

c. Click the Copy SmartIcon. The information is copied to the Clipboard.

d. Now move to the CHAIRS worksheet. Move the cell pointer to the cell immediately below the Dinette entry in the Description column.

e. Click the Paste SmartIcon. Lotus 1-2-3 copies the information from the UPDATE worksheet into the CHAIRS worksheet.

f. Make any formatting enhancements needed to make the new entries look consistent with the original worksheet data.

g. Save and print a copy of the revised CHAIRS worksheet.

INDEPENDENTCHALLENGE

You are an operations manager at Good Step Shoes. One of your responsibilities is to prepare a forecasted income statement for the company's line of men's shoes. Typically, the marketing manager provides you with a forecasted marketing expense report, and the office manager provides you with a forecasted administrative expense report. Once you receive the two reports, you review the data and include it in your forecasted income statement.

Plan and build a marketing expenses worksheet file and an administrative expenses worksheet file, then copy and move the expense totals from the source worksheets to a final income worksheet file. Enter your own forecast data, but use the following guidelines.

- Expense forecasts at Good Step Shoes are listed by quarter (Q1, Q2, Q3, Q4). Use formulas or functions to calculate quarterly expense totals as well as a grand total.

- Marketing expenses often include items such as advertising, travel, entertainment, and supplies.

- Administrative expenses often include items such as clerical salaries, office supplies, postage, and utilities.

- The income statement should list a yearly sales projection, from which items such as cost of goods sold, marketing expenses, and administrative expenses are subtracted. This results in a forecasted net income statement.

To complete this independent challenge:

1 Prepare a worksheet plan that states your goal, lists the worksheet data you'll need, identifies the multiple worksheet files you'll need to build, and specifies formulas or functions you'll need to use.

2 Sketch a sample worksheet on a piece of paper, indicating how the information should be organized. What data can you copy or move from file to file?

3 Build the worksheet files with your own forecast data. Enter the titles and labels first, then enter the numbers and formulas. Save the worksheet files as MARKET, ADMIN, and INCOME, respectively.

4 Make enhancements to the INCOME worksheet. Format labels and values, change attributes and alignment, and add borders. Also, remember to check your spelling.

5 Before printing, preview the files so you know what the worksheets will look like. Adjust any items as needed, and print a copy of each. Save your work before closing files.

6 Submit your worksheet plan, preliminary sketches, and final worksheet printouts.

UNIT 9

Automating
WORKSHEET TASKS

macro automatically performs a task or sequence of tasks and can be used in worksheets, charts, and database tables. You create macros to automate Lotus 1-2-3 tasks that you perform frequently and that require a series of steps. For example, if you usually type your name and date in a worksheet, Lotus 1-2-3 can memorize the keystrokes needed to do this in a macro. In this unit, you will learn how to plan and design a simple macro, and you will record, name, and run a macro. ▶ Jim Howard from the Tours Department wants to create a macro that will quickly adjust column widths. ▶

Planning a macro

A macro is a single instruction that performs several different commands in a sequence determined by the user. A macro can enter and format text, for instance, or save and print a worksheet. Most tasks that you perform on a regular basis can be made into macros. ▶ In Lotus 1-2-3 you can create a macro by recording a series of actions or by writing the instructions in a specific format. Since the sequence of actions is important, you need to plan the macro carefully before you create it. Commands used to create, run, and modify macros are located on the Macro submenu of the Tools menu. ▶ Jim Howard finds that he often needs to adjust column widths to fit the largest entry and decides to create a macro to do this. Jim reviews the steps he uses to perform this task.

■ Give the planned macro a descriptive name and write out a description of what it should do

Jim decides to call the macro Wide Column and writes the description "Adjusts column to fit widest entry," as shown in Figure 9-1.

■ Decide how to execute the commands you are recording

Jim decides to use the mouse to click menus open and click commands.

■ Practice the steps you want Lotus 1-2-3 to memorize and write them down

Jim writes down the sequence of actions. Jim is now ready to record and test the macro.

■ Decide where to locate the description of the macro and the macro itself. Macros may be stored either in an unused area of a worksheet or grouped together in another worksheet.

Jim decides to store the macro in the far right side of the worksheet.

FIGURE 9-1: Paper description of planned macro

Macro to Adjust Column Widths

Name: Wide Column

Description: Adjusts column to fit
                widest entry

Steps: Click Style on the menu bar
                Click Column Width
                Click Fit widest entry
                Click OK

Standard macro commands

Lotus 1-2-3 comes with many preset commands to help you build macros. To view a list of these commands, type **{**, then press **[F3]**. To enter a macro command into a worksheet, click **OK**. To complete the macro you will need to type the cell addresses or ranges that will be modified by the macro. Type **}** to end the macro. Lotus 1-2-3 also comes with a worksheet, UIMACROS.WK4, that contains macros. Use these macros or combine them to build more complex macros.

Recording a macro

Recording is the easiest way to create a macro. As you record, each action is listed on the Transcript window, which you can view by selecting it from the Macro submenu. To begin recording, use the Record command on the Macro submenu, then complete the tasks normally. When finished, use the Stop Recording command. After recording, you can select the sequences from the Transcript window and define them as macros. ▶ Jim Howard wants to create a macro that will allow him to quickly resize columns to fit the widest cell entry. He will create this macro by recording his actions.

1 Open the worksheet UNIT_9-1.WK4, then save it as COLMACR1

2 Click **Tools** on the menu bar, then click **Macro**, then click **Record**

3 Select the range **A1..M1**, click **Style** on the menu bar, then click **Column Width**
   All of your actions will be recorded as part of the macro.

4 Click **Fit widest entry**, then click **OK**
   When applied, the macro will resize the selected columns so that each is as wide as its widest cell contents.

5 Click **Tools** on the menu bar, than click **Macro**, then click **Stop Recording**
   "Rec" no longer displays in the status bar. Lotus 1-2-3 stops recording your actions.

6 Click **Tools** on the menu bar, then click **Macro**, then click **Show Transcript**
   The Transcript window displays all of the actions you made while recording, as shown in Figure 9-2. Save your work and continue to the next lesson without closing the worksheet.

FIGURE 9-2: Worksheet and Transcript window

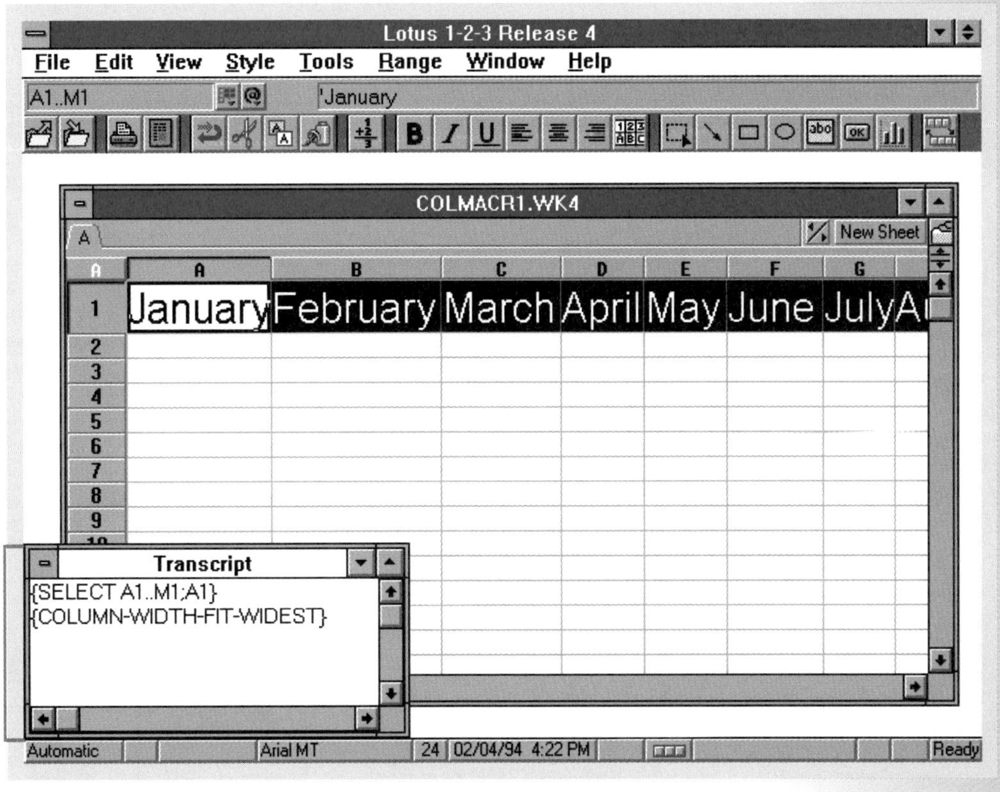

All recorded actions display in the Transcript window

Creating multiple macros

It is possible to create several macros from one recording session. Choose Record from the Macro submenu and work normally. When finished, stop recording and scroll through the Transcript window. Copy each useful sequence and create a macro for it. By reviewing the actions of an entire work session, you will be able to identify repetitive tasks that could be accomplished more efficiently with macros. The contents of the Transcript window are erased when you exit Lotus 1-2-3.

TROUBLE?

If you make a mistake while recording a macro, click Stop Recording in the Macros Submenu and start again■

Naming a macro

After you have recorded actions that will be made into a macro, you need to copy the sequence of actions from the Transcript window to the worksheet. Then, assign the macro a range name in order to run the macro. When naming a macro, use the Name command from the Range menu to name the first cell of the macro. Table 9-1 lists some of the guidelines for naming ranges. ▶ Jim Howard has decided to name the macro WideColumn.

1 Select the contents of the **Transcript window**, then click the **Copy SmartIcon** 🔲

Lotus 1-2-3 copies the sequence of actions to the Clipboard. Now you are ready to paste the sequence into an unused portion of the worksheet.

2 Click cell **P2**, then click the **Paste SmartIcon** 🔳

Lotus 1-2-3 places the sequence in the worksheet. It's a good idea to identify, or document, macro commands so that you can easily determine the purpose of each command. Now Jim wants to identify the macro by giving it a name.

3 Click cell **P1** and type **WideColumn**, then press **[Enter]**

Compare your worksheet with Figure 9-3. Now you are ready to use the Name command from the Range menu.

4 Select the macro sequence in the range P2..R2, then click **Range** on the menu bar, then click **Name**

Lotus 1-2-3 displays the Name dialog box. Assigning a name to a macro enables you to run it later, using the Run command.

5 Type **WideColumn** in the Name text box

Macro names should be descriptive.

6 Click **Add**, then click **OK**

WideColumn appears in the list of named ranges.

7 Save your work and continue to the next lesson without closing the worksheet

TABLE 9-1:
Range naming guidelines

SUBJECT	GUIDELINE
Length of name	Use up to 15 characters
Case	Use uppercase, lowercase, or mixed cases; Lotus 1-2-3 displays name in uppercase
Name	Avoid names that look like cell addresses, function names, or names of keys
Punctuation	May not be used as the first character
Numbers	May not be used as the first character
Spaces	May not be used; use underscores or hyphens

FIGURE 9-3: Worksheet with macro and description

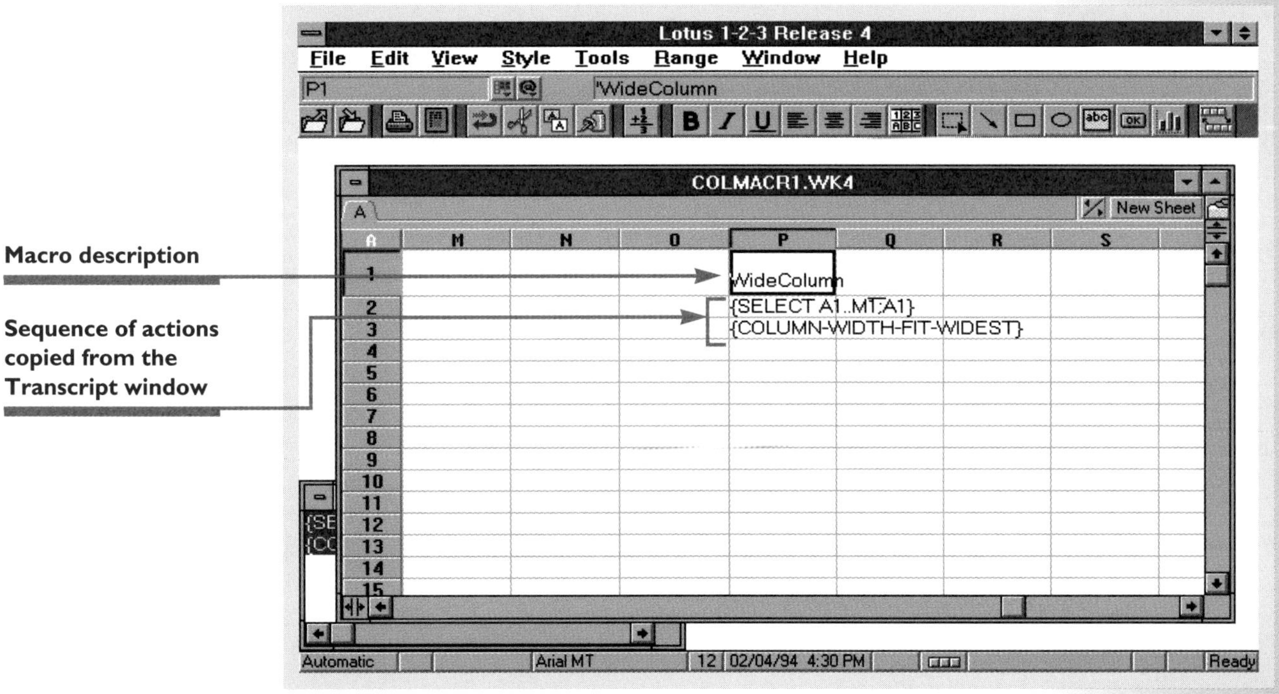

Macro description

Sequence of actions copied from the Transcript window

Running an unnamed macro

You might want to test-drive a macro by running it before you assign a name with the Name command. To run an unnamed macro, select the first cell of a macro sequence, click Tools on the menu bar, then click Macro Run, then click OK.

TROUBLE?

If you create a macro for one range and apply it to another, it will not run. You need to adjust the range and then run the macro.■

Running a macro

To run a macro, you must choose the Run command from the Macro submenu and choose the named macro you want. If a macro was designed to affect a specific range of cells, and you want to use it to affect a different range, you will need to alter the macro. ▶Jim Howard has recorded and named a macro to adjust column widths to fit the largest entry in the COLMACR1 worksheet. He needs to change the formatting of the worksheet and readjust column widths. Now try running this macro to see how it adjusts the worksheet.

1 Select the range **A1..L1**, click **Style** on the menu bar, then click **Font & Attributes**, click **Size 12**, then click **OK**
The labels are reduced to 12 points, and the columns need to be resized.

2 Click **Tools** on the menu bar, then click **Macro,** then click **Run**
The Macro Run dialog box displays, as shown in Figure 9-4.

3 Click **WIDECOLUMN** in the **All named ranges list box,** then click **OK**
Columns A1..L1 are resized automatically.

4 Click the **Save File SmartIcon** 📇 then close your worksheet

FIGURE 9-4: Worksheet with Macro Run dialog box

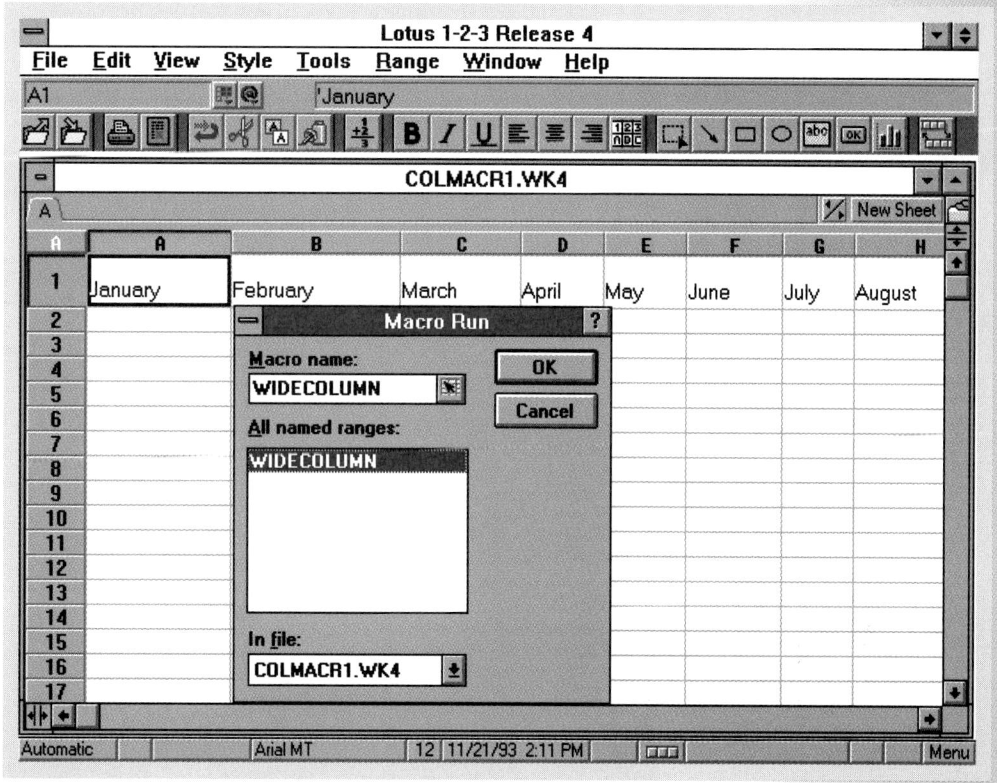

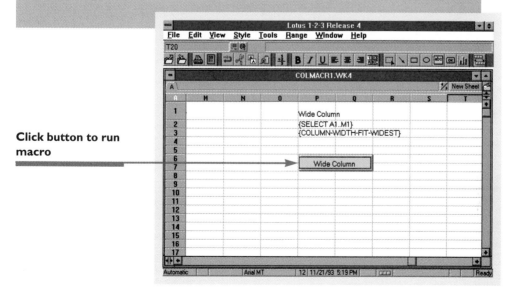

Assigning a macro to a button

You can make macros even easier to use by assigning a button to run a macro. After you create a macro, draw a button with the Draw Button command from the Tools menu. Then assign a macro to the button by using the Assign to Button dialog box. You can add color and text to customize the appearance of the macro button, as shown in Figure 9-5.

Click button to run macro

FIGURE 9-5: Worksheet with macro button

QUICK TIP

Macros with the prefix \0 (backslash zero) run every time a worksheet is opened.

CONCEPTSREVIEW

Label each of the elements of the macro shown in Figure 9-6

1 _____

2 _____

3 _____

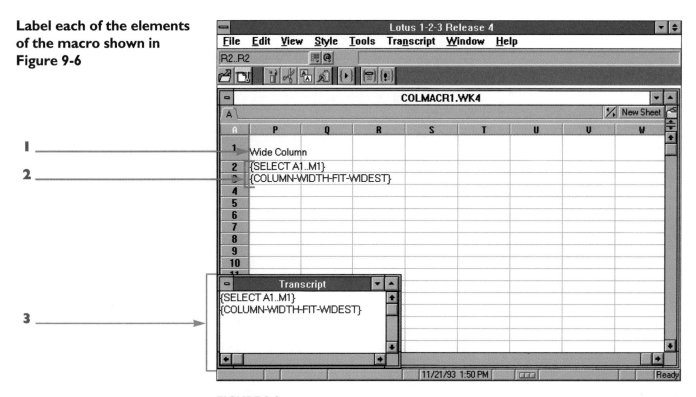

FIGURE 9-6

Select the best answer from the list of choices.

4 Which of the following would be the best candidate for a macro?

a. Simple commands

b. Often-used sequences of commands or actions

c. Seldom-used commands or tasks

d. Nonsequential tasks

5 To name a macro, you:

a. Type the name on the worksheet

b. Use the Name Macro command

c. Use the Name command from the Range menu

d. Create a button

6 The best place to store a macro on a worksheet is:

a. The area of the worksheet used for values

b. An unused area to the far right or well below the worksheet contents

c. A worksheet that contains only macros

d. On a custom Work menu

7 All of following guidelines apply to naming a macro, EXCEPT:

a. Name may contain up to 15 characters

b. Name may not contain punctuation as the first character

c. Name should not resemble cell address

d. Name may contain spaces

8 The Transcript window contains:

a. All the macros that are stored in a worksheet

b. Actions performed since the Record command was activated

c. A list of all macros associated with the current worksheet

d. The name of the macro being recorded

9 Which of the following actions would not run a macro?

a. Clicking a macro button

b. Choosing Run from the Macro submenu

c. Opening a worksheet with macros containing /0

d. Choosing Execute Macro from the Tools menu

APPLICATIONS REVIEW

1 On paper, plan a macro that will enter and format labels for the 12 months of the year.

a. The labels will be entered in A1..N1.

b. The labels will be each of the twelve months (January, February, etc.)

c. The labels will be 14-point Times.

d. The macro will be named EnterMonths.

2 Record the EnterMonths macro.

a. Open a new worksheet and name it Months.

b. Click Record on the Macro submenu to begin recording.

c. Type in the labels.

d. Format the labels (14-point Times).

e. Stop recording.

3 Copy the contents of the Transcript window to the worksheet.

a. Type the name and description of the macro in A15.

b. Open the Transcript window.

c. Copy the contents of the Transcript window.

d. Paste the contents below A15.

e. Compare your results with Figure 9-7.

f. Make any adjustments, then save your work.

4 Name the macro.

a. Select the macro command.

b. Use the Name command from the Range menu and type the name EnterMonths.

c. Save your work.

5 Test the EnterMonths macro.

a. Delete the contents of A1..N1.

b. On the Macro submenu, click run, then click ENTERMONTHS.

c. If the macro does not run correctly, review each step.

d. Save your work, then close the worksheet.

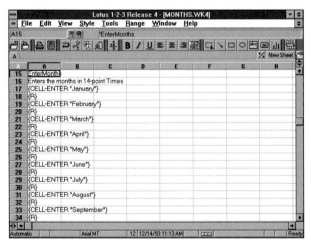

FIGURE 9-7

INDEPENDENTCHALLENGE

You are a new employee for a manufacturer of computer software. Your responsibility is to track the sales of different product lines and find out which types of computers sell the most software each month.

You need to streamline the way the sales are calculated and inserted on the worksheet used to create the report. The information will be contained in a worksheet file that contains worksheet windows for Summary, Games, Business, and Utilities. Each worksheet window will track the sales of programs for DOS, Windows, and Macintosh computers. You will need to incorporate the information from the following table.

Summary			
Product	**DOS**	**Windows**	**Macintosh**
Games	The information in this window will be auto-entered when the totals are calculated.		
Business			
Utilities			

Games			
Product	**DOS**	**Windows**	**Macintosh**
Space Wars 456	789	640	
Safari	230	400	800
Flight School	330	120	1,000

Business			
Product	**DOS**	**Windows**	**Macintosh**
Word processing	12,345	4,567	3,470
Spreadsheet	7,899	3,450	4,567
Presentation	4,590	6,789	12,345
Graphics	8,902	4,321	4,200
Page layout	350	5,690	8,975

Utilities			
Product	**DOS**	**Windows**	**Macintosh**
Antivirus	4,567	4,010	2,314
File recovery	6,789	5,678	3, 467

To complete this independent challenge:

1 Create a new worksheet called SOFTWARE and insert and name worksheet windows for Summary, Games, Business, and Utilities.

2 Create a macro that will enter the labels Product, DOS, Windows, Macintosh

3 Create a macro that will add the sales for each product line.

4 Change the macro so that it will run on all of the worksheet windows. Remember that the different product lines have different numbers of products.

5 Create a macro that will enter the totals from each worksheet window on the summary sheet. Hint: You will insert the sum of a named range on the Summary sheet window; for example, @SUM(Utilities B6). Name the macro InsertTotal.

6 Print your work.

7 Submit your final worksheet printouts, including the macros and their descriptions.

Glossary

Absolute reference　A cell reference that contains a dollar sign before the column letter and/or row number to indicate the absolute, or fixed, contents of specific cells. For example, the formula A1+B1 calculates only the sum of these specific cells.

Address　The location of a specific cell or range expressed by the coordinates of column and row; for example, A1.

Alignment　The horizontal placement of cell contents; for example, left, center, or right.

Append records　A command that adds records to a database.

Application　A software program, such as Lotus 1-2-3 or WordPerfect that enables you to perform a certain type of task, such as data calculations or word processing.

Area chart　A line chart in which each area is given a solid color or pattern to emphasize the relationships between the pieces of charted information.

Argument　A value, range of cells, or text used in a macro or @function. An argument is enclosed in parentheses; for example, @SUM(A1..B1).

Attribute　The styling features such as bold, italics, and underlining that may be applied to cell contents.

Background color　The color applied to the background of a cell.

Bar chart　The default chart type in Lotus 1-2-3. The bar chart displays information as a series of columns.

Border　The outside edge of a selected area of a worksheet. Lines and color may be applied to borders.

Cancel button　The X on the Edit line; the Cancel button removes information from the Contents box and leaves a blank cell or restores the previous cell entry.

Cascading menu　A subgroup of related commands that appear to the right side of a pull-down menu.

Cell　The intersection of a row and column.

Cell pointer　A highlighted rectangle around a cell that indicates where in a worksheet you are currently working.

Cell reference　The address or name of a specific cell; cell references may be absolute or relative.

Chart　A graphic representation of selected worksheet information. Types include bar, pie, area, and line charts.

Chart title　The name assigned to a chart.

Clear　A command used to erase a cell's contents, formatting, or both.

Clipboard　A temporary storage area for items that have been copied and that may be pasted.

Close　A command that puts a file away without saving it but keeps Lotus 1-2-3 open so that you can continue to work on other worksheets.

Confirm button　The check mark on the Edit line; the confirm button is used to confirm an entry.

Contents box　The rectangular area on the Edit line that displays a cell's contents, including numbers, text, and formulas, when you click a cell.

Control menu box　A box in the upper-left corner of a window used to resize or close a window.

Copy　A command that copies the selected information and places it on the Clipboard.

Copy down　A command that duplicates the contents of the selected cells in the range selected below the cell pointer.

Copy right　A command that duplicates the contents of the selected cells in the range selected to the right of the cell pointer.

Criteria　The information a user wants Lotus 1-2-3 to compare with the contents of a database or worksheet. Criteria are used with the Find & Replace, Delete Record, Find Record, and other commands. Criteria are also used to create query tables.

Cut　A command that removes the contents from a selected area of a worksheet and places them on the Clipboard.

Data series   The selected range in a worksheet that Lotus 1-2-3 converts into a graphic and displays as a chart.

Database   A collection of information organized by fields and records. A telephone book, a card catalog, and a list of company employees are all databases.

Database table   A range of a worksheet that organizes information into fields and records.

Delete   A command that removes cell contents from a worksheet.

Delete records   A command that removes records from a database.

Dialog box   A window that displays when you choose a command whose name is followed by an ellipsis (…). A dialog box allows you to make selections that determine how the command affects the selected area.

Directory   A section of a disk used to store specific information, much like a folder in a file cabinet.

Drag and drop   A way of moving or copying cells, rows, and columns by dragging the data with the mouse to a new worksheet location.

Drives   A disk or area of a network used for storing files. Drives are organized by directories.

Edit   A change made to the contents of a cell or worksheet.

Edit line   The area below the title bar and above the Lotus 1-2-3 workspace. The Edit line provides information about the contents of the current cell.

Electronic spreadsheet   A computer program that performs calculations on data and organizes information. A spreadsheet is divided into rows and columns that form individual cells.

Field   A labeled column in a database table; it contains the same kind of information for each record, such as a phone number.

Find   A command used to locate information the use specifies.

Find & Replace   A command used to find one set of criteria and replace it with new information.

Font   The typeface used to display information in cells.

Format   The appearance of text and numbers, including color, font, attributes, and worksheet defaults. See also *number format*.

Formula   A set of instructions that you enter in a cell to perform numeric calculations (adding, multiplying, averaging, etc.); for example, +A1+B1.

Function   A special predefined formula that provides a shortcut for commonly used calculations; for example, @AVG.

Function selector   A menu on the Edit line that lists common Lotus 1-2-3 functions.

Icon   A picture or symbol that represents a command or identifies an object on the Windows desktop.

Label   Descriptive text or other information that identify the rows and columns of a worksheet. Labels are not included in calculations.

Label prefix   A character that identifies an entry as a label and controls the way it is displayed in the cell.

Launch   Start a software program so you can use it.

Legend   A key explaining the information represented by colors or patterns in a chart.

Line chart   A graph of data that is mapped by a series of lines. Line charts show changes in data or categories of data over time and can be used to document trends.

Macro   A set of recorded instructions that tell the computer to perform a task or series of tasks.

Menu bar   The area under the title bar on a window. The menu bar provides access to most of an application's commands.

Mode indicator   A box located on the bottom-left of the status bar that informs you of the program's status. For example, when Lotus 1-2-3 is performing a task, the word "Wait" displays.

Mouse pointer   An arrow that indicates the current location of the mouse on the desktop. The mouse pointer changes shapes at times; for example, when you insert data, select a range, position a chart, change the size of a window, or select a topic in Help.

Number format   A format applied to values to express numerical concepts, such as currency, date, and percent.

Open   A command that retrieves a worksheet from a disk and displays it on the screen.

Operator   A symbol used in formulas, such as + or −.

Order of operations   The order in which Lotus 1-2-3 calculates parts of a formula: (1) exponents, (2) multiplication and division, and (3) addition and subtraction.

Paste   A command that moves information on the Clipboard to a new location. Lotus 1-2-3 pastes the formulas, rather than the result unless the Paste Special command is used.

Paste special   A command that enables you to paste formulas as values, styles, or cell contents.

Perspective view   A mode in which Lotus 1-2-3 displays up to three worksheet windows at a time.

Pie chart   A circular chart that displays data as slices of a pie. A pie chart is useful for showing the relationship of parts to a whole.

Point   A unit of measure used for fonts and row height. One inch equals 72 points.

Print Preview   Reduced view of area to be printed.

Program Manager   The main control program of Windows. All Windows applications are started from the Program Manager.

Pull-down menu   A group of related commands located under a single word on the menu bar. For example, basic commands (New, Open, Save, Close, and Print), are grouped on the File menu.

Random Access Memory (RAM)   A temporary storage area in a computer that is erased each time the computer is turned off or whenever there is a fluctuation in power. When a program is launched, it is loaded into RAM so you can work with that program.

Range   A selected area of adjacent cells.

Range format   A format applied to a selected range in a worksheet.

Range name   A name applied to a selected range in a worksheet.

Record   Horizontal rows in the database table that contain information that pertains to a subject.

Record   One way to create macros; the Record command memorizes all actions you want a macro to perform.

Relative cell reference   Used by Lotus 1-2-3 to indicate a relative position in the worksheet. This allows you to copy and move formulas from one area to another of the same dimensions. Lotus 1-2-3 automatically changes the column and row numbers to reflect the new position.

Row height   The vertical dimension of a cell.

Run   Execute a macro.

Save   A command used to save incremental changes to a worksheet.

Save As   A command used to create a duplicate of the current worksheet.

Scroll bars   Bars that appear on the right and bottom borders of the worksheet window to give you access to information not currently visible on the screen.

Selection indicator   The leftmost area on th Edit line that shows the name or address of the area currently selected. For example, B:A1 refers to cell A1 on the second worksheet window.

SmartIcon   A picture that represents a shortcut for performing a variety of Lotus 1-2-3 tasks. For example, you can click the Save SmartIcon to save a file. The SmartIcon palette is located beneath the Edit line.

SmartIcon selector button   A button on the status bar that allows you to select other sets of SmartIcons and to customize the position of SmartIcons.

Sort   To arrange contents of a database or selected range in a particular sequence.

Sort key   Any cell in a field by which a database or selected range is being sorted.

Spell check   A command that attempts to match all text in a worksheet with the words in the Lotus 1-2-3 dictionary.

Status bar   The bar at the bottom of the screen that provides information about the tasks Lotus 1-2-3 is performing or about any current selections.

Title bar   The bar at the top of a window that displays the name given a worksheet when it is saved and named.

Transcript window   A window that stores all the actions you make when the Record command is chosen from the Macro submenu. You create macros by pasting these actions into a worksheet.

Window   A framed area of a screen. Each worksheet occupies a window.

Worksheet tab   A worksheet letter in the top left corner of the worksheet that identifies each worksheet window in a file.

Worksheet window   The area where you place all calculations; a worksheet window is a grid of up to 256 columns and 8,192 rows.

X-axis   The horizontal line in a chart.

X-axis label   A label describing the x-axis of a chart.

Y-axis   The vertical line in a chart.

Y-axis label   A label describing the y-axis of a chart.

Zoom in   A SmartIcon function that enables you to focus on a smaller part of the worksheet in Print Preview by enlarging it.

Zoom out   A SmartIcon function that enables you to view a larger part of the worksheet in Print Preview by shrinking it.

Index

Because you purchased this Course Technology textbook, you are eligible for a special value. You can purchase the Lotus 1-2-3 Release 4.01 for Windows software for just $34.95 plus shipping.

Now you can get your own copy of Lotus 1-2-3 Release 4.01 for Windows in a special version designed for students.

Important: Please read the information below before ordering

System Requirements

- An 80286, 80386, or 80486-based computer certified for use with Microsoft Windows 3.1 or later
- A color or grayscale EGA, VGA, or IBM 8514 monitor

  If your computer displays VGA colors in grayscale, use Windows Setup to choose the appropriate color driver
- A mouse is strongly recommended

  You must use the mouse to select individual chart elements, or collections, or multiple drawn objects. You also need the mouse to begin drawing, moving, or sizing a drawn object; and to use SmartIcons, the status bar, and worksheet tabs.
- Microsoft Windows 3.1 or later and DOS 3.30 or later
- Four megabytes (MB) of Random Access Memory(RAM); use on an 80286-based computer might require more RAM

  A 2MB or more swap file is recommended in 386 enhanced mode.
- A minimum of 7.5MB of available disk space

Note

The Student Version of Lotus 1-2-3 Release 4.01 for Windows is a fully operational version of the software but with reduced functionality. It does not include Tools Audit, Spell Check, Lotus Dialog Editor, Translate Utility, Macro Translator, Detailed Macro Help, Detailed @Function Help, Guided Tour, Online Tutorial, DataLens drivers, or Version Manager for Notes. All printouts include the words "Printed with the Student Version of 1-2-3" at the bottom of the page. Product/software support is provided.

See reverse side for details

Please send me Lotus 1-2-3 Release 4.01 for Windows student software

See reverse side for details

I have enclosed all of the following:

- This original coupon (no photocopies or reproductions please).

- A photocopy of my current student ID.

- A check or money order for $39.95 ($34.95 plus $5.00 shipping). Massachusetts residents must add $1.75 for sales tax. For rush handling (delivery in 5 to 10 days), add $7.50 (for a total of $47.45) and check here: ☐

You must include this original coupon, full payment, and a photocopy of your student ID. Incomplete orders will be returned. No credit card orders. Maximum one software order per person. For your own protection, do not send currency through the mail. Allow 4 to 6 weeks for normal delivery. All units are shipped on 3.5-inch disks.

Make check payable to **Course Technology, Inc.**

Name _____

Address _____

_____

City _____

State_____ **Zip** _____

Telephone _____

School _____

Send to:
Lotus 1-2-3 Student Upgrade Program
Course Technology, Inc.
One Main St.
Cambridge, MA 02142